Napoleon Hill's
Keys to Positive Thinking

Napoleon Hill's
Keys to Positive Thinking

10 STEPS TO HEALTH, WEALTH, AND SUCCESS

Napoleon Hill and Michael J. Ritt, Jr.

Published by: The Napoleon Hill Foundation
PO Box 1277
Wise, VA 24293

Website: www.naphill.org
Email: napoleonhill@uvawise.edu

ISBN: 0-937539-85-6

Distributed by: Executive Books
206 W. Allen Street
Mechanicsburg, PA 17055

Telephone: 800-233-2665
Website: www.executivebooks.com

Contents

ACKNOWLEDGMENTS

In a letter to English scientist Robert Hooke, Sir Isaac Newton wrote, "If I have seen further [than Hooke and Descartes], it is by standing upon the shoulders of giants." So it is for me. If I presume to tell you about principles and practices that can change your life, it is because my own life has been altered by giants who have permitted me to observe the world from astride their shoulders.

I refer first to William James, M.D., the psychologist and philosopher. Though I did not know the man, it was he who provided a strong theoretical foundation for a Positive Mental Attitude (PMA). Second, I point you to Napoleon Hill, that extraordinary seeker of the secrets of success, who was the first to quantify the principles of PMA and reveal his findings in self-help books. I knew and worked with Napoleon Hill for almost twenty valuable years. And third, I acknowledge my debt to W. Clement Stone, giant of giants, who has striven tirelessly to teach others what he has put into practice so successfully himself—the amazing power of a Positive Mental Attitude.

—Michael J. Ritt

Introduction

You can change your life with this small book. It contains the key to your success: PMA, positive mental attitude. You can achieve PMA and realize your dreams when you follow the proven principles outlined simply and clearly in this step-by-step guide.

A View of the Promised Land

In the Bible we are told that just before Moses reached the end of his life, God led him up to the top of Mount Nebo and showed the great leader the land that was going to belong to the Israelites. Before you begin this journey to take charge of your life, you, too, deserve a vision of where you are going. You are coming to the end of an old way of living and are soon to embark on a new beginning. Starting now, you will be casting off old, energy-draining, negative ways of looking at the world and replacing them with the irresistibly invigorating life that comes with a Positive Mental Attitude. Carry this image of hope with you—the hope of what PMA will do for you. Imagine, from this day on:

- You will recognize that you have a God-given creative power within you.
- You will develop control of your emotions so that you can always direct their creative power for your own good.
- You will eliminate all the negative attitudes that have resulted from your ineffective reaction to past experiences.
- You will overcome your fears, realizing that they have a destructive influence upon your creative power if you permit them to dominate your mind.
- You will picture only good things happening to you so that this creative power will be expressed only within a good and positive framework.
- You will stop brooding over your past failures and tragedies and stop causing them to be repeated in your life.
- You will direct your strongest feelings and desires toward the things you truly want in life.
- You will never knowingly use the creative power of PMA for selfish or evil purposes, knowing that the misuse of it can cause it to destroy you and all that you value.

Attaining these benefits (your birthright as a human being) will be your goal from this day on. Nothing can stop you, and the only resource you need is your own commitment to making them happen.

1

What Will PMA Do for You?

A Positive Mental Attitude allows you to build on hope and overcome despair and discouragement. By developing and possessing PMA, you will find your state of mind is consistently wholesome, healthy, and productive in your reactions to other people and in choosing actions that will lead you to whatever worthy things you want in life. It is no wonder that PMA is called the "I CAN—I WILL" philosophy.

When you have PMA, you are happy with yourself—and with others. You will possess that inner air, that inner light, that inner feeling that allows you to have self-respect and beneficial feelings. You will attract good-will and circumstances and repel negative ones.

The effects of PMA are automatic, but attaining it is not. PMA requires a continual process of application. It is not something to use at your convenience. It is an essential part of the way you live. PMA must become a *habit* with you, so ingrained that you demonstrate it always. By regular application of PMA, you can practice it without conscious thought, the way you button a button or tie your shoes. It must and can be as natural as breathing. As a road sign in upper New York State once said, "Choose your rut carefully; you'll be in it for the next ten miles."

Nothing Succeeds Like Success . . .

Whom would you rather spend time with?

- Someone who is pessimistic, suspicious, sullen, and always sure that the only cloud in the sky heralds a hurricane?
- Someone who is optimistic, confident, gregarious, and always able to tackle a problem, find a solution, and maximize the benefits?

You can see why PMA allows you to win the friendship and cooperation of other people, to overcome any obstacle, and to turn problems into opportunities.

We are all ruled by our habits. Whether your habits and their effects are positive or negative depends on your choices. You can choose not to allow your mind to be dominated by negative thoughts. You can make a conscious decision to replace negative ideas and impulses

A PMA allows you to turn (potential) adversity into potential success.

with positive ones whenever they occur. Positive habits will automatically influence your mind to be more alert, your imagination to be more active, your enthusiasm to grow, and your willpower to increase.

PMA attracts its benefits like a magnet attracts iron filings. PMA will attract people, success, and wealth to you. An optimistic outlook is irresistible. PMA shields and protects you from doubts and hopelessness. When adversity comes into your life—and it visits us all—you will be protected from despair and prevented from being overwhelmed by circumstances. In fact, PMA allows you to see any situation more clearly, so that you can turn adversity into potential success by learning from it and using that knowledge to your benefit.

PMA is the correct mental response to any incoming stimulus from your senses. With PMA at your command, you think about, act upon, or react to each person or circumstance in the right way. Your mind and your life are yours to do with as you deem appropriate.

PMA teaches you to think and act constructively. You can use PMA to bring your wants and desires into reality. When you learn to make the best of what you have, you learn to seize opportunity where others see only a problem. You can put into practice the philosophy of Benjamin Disraeli, the great British Prime Minister: "We are not creatures of circumstance; we are creators of circumstance."

One way to train yourself to act with PMA is to select a *self-motivator*, a word or phrase that is meaningful to you and reminds you of your commitment to PMA and the goals you are pursuing. By recalling it to memory often, especially when you find yourself confronting a situation in which PMA is especially called for, you strengthen your resolve to act in the most appropriate manner possible.

Choosing a Self-Motivator

You want a self-motivator that reinforces the key aspects of PMA in your life. If you know you have a particular attitude that you want to overcome, you can tailor your self-motivator to address it.

Because your self-motivator will become such an integral part of your life, choose one that reflects your noblest convictions. In this way you will be reminded and inspired always to act in conformity with them. Your goal is to become a *congruent* person—making the person you say you are and the person you really are the same.

Some suggestions:

Do unto others as you would have others do unto you.

I feel healthy, I feel happy, I feel terrific.

Do it now!

What I can conceive and believe, I can achieve.

Every problem contains the seed of its own solution.

How, not if.

Victory is won in inches, not miles.

I can. I will.

Repeat your self-motivator aloud many times throughout the day. Say it with feeling and emotion fifty times before you go to bed. Post it where you can see it: on the mirror in the bathroom, on the dashboard of your car, on your desk calendar, on the refrigerator door, in your wallet. The more you repeat it, the more it and the values it expresses become a habit.

Some Who Nourished PMA

Many people contributed to the development and refinement of the PMA concept. William James (1842–1910), a Harvard Medical School graduate who stayed at the university to teach anatomy, physiology, psychology, and philosophy, helped to develop a system of thought called *pragmatism*. According to the ideas of pragmatism, results are what count. Thought is a guide to action. If a thought does not result in practical actions, it is not useful. James wrote, "Be not afraid of life. Believe that life is worth living, and your belief will create the fact."

The people of James's day respected his theories, and he attracted many followers. He was convinced that life is a battle between pessimism and optimism. James vehemently opposed negative thinking. "It fill[s] people with failure and doubt," he said. The universe, according to James, was full of *possibilities*. People could vastly improve themselves if they only opened their eyes and looked for the mind power they had within them. James believed that each of us decides what our future will be and that, "We become what we think about most of the time. The greatest revolution in our generation is the discovery that human beings, by changing the inner attitudes of their minds, can change the outer aspects of their lives."

Napoleon Hill (1883–1970) was another who carried the PMA baton. Hill made it his life work to interview immensely successful people, deriving seventeen principles from this study that he wove into the first practical philosophy of personal achievement. Hill enumerated these principles in various books, including *The Law of Success, Think and Grow Rich*, and many other self-help books. Hill always found that the men he studied shared a Positive Mental Attitude. He noted about one, "Andrew Carnegie had an obsession. He believed that anything in life worth having was worth working for. I believe that anything in life worth having and working for is worth paying for."

Willye White, Olympic silver medalist, believes it too. She is the motivator behind Chicago's Robert Taylor Homes Girls Athletic Program. The program offers 2,500 girls who live in Chicago's south side public housing complex a way to improve their self-esteem through athletics. When the girls ask White how they can get out of the grips of life in public housing, she tells them, "There are ways. Now, my question to you is: what price are you willing to pay for your dreams? A dream without a plan is only a wish!" (Their self-motivator: BELIEVE IT, ACHIEVE IT!)

W. Clement Stone, a man I worked with for nearly

fifty years, an outstanding contemporary author and a man who accumulated and shared his great wealth by using and mastering these principles, made a profound discovery while coauthoring (with Napoleon Hill) the book *Success Through a Positive Mental Attitude*. The essence of his discovery was this: the basic principles of success are effective in achieving worthwhile goals only to the extent that they are constantly reinforced and replenished by a Positive Mental Attitude.

That principle became the cornerstone of Stone's philosophy and the theme that unified his writings. The stage was set, and PMA dominated the spotlight. As the examples throughout this book will show you, PMA is still the hallmark of every person who has achieved lasting success.

What Is PMA?

PMA stands for Positive Mental Attitude, but PMA is more than just an optimistic outlook on life. When you understand it thoroughly and apply it correctly, you will see that it is, in effect, a fourfold process. It consists of:

1. an honest, well-balanced way of thinking;
2. a successful consciousness;
3. an all-embracing philosophy of living; and
4. the ability to follow through with the correct actions and reactions.

Napoleon Hill defined a Positive Mental Attitude this way: it is "a confident, honest, constructive state of mind which an individual creates and maintains by methods of his own choosing, through the operation of his own willpower, based on the motives of his own adaptation."

W. Clement Stone added: "A Positive Mental Attitude is the *right* honest thought, action, or reaction to a given situation or set of circumstances, i.e., thoughts, actions, and reactions which do not violate the laws of God or the right of your fellow man, for those who have PMA."

Stone has explained further: "You are the product of your heredity, environment, physical body, conscious and subconscious mind, particular position, and direction in time and space, and something more, including powers known and unknown. When you think with PMA, you can affect, use, control, harmonize with, or neutralize any or all of these factors. You can direct your thoughts, control your emotions, and ordain your destiny. You are a mind with a body."

So what is PMA? Examine the meaning of the three words that form the concept of Positive Mental Attitude:

POSITIVE. PMA is a force or power associated with "plus" characteristics such as honesty, faith, love, integrity, hope, optimism, courage, initiative, generosity, diligence, kindliness, and good common sense.

MENTAL. PMA is a power of your mind, not of your body. Remember, "You are a MIND with a body." Your control is embodied within your mind.

ATTITUDE. PMA depends on the right attitudes, which are feelings or moods. Attitude relates to your basic feelings toward yourself, another person, situation, circumstance, or thing.

The three initial letters combined—PMA—stand for the term Positive Mental Attitude, the adhesive that binds all your plus characteristics, the power source that enables you to be a person who can achieve anything and everything so long as what you desire or do does not violate the laws of God or infringe upon the rights of others. Simply stated, Positive Mental Attitude is the right frame of mind that leads inevitably to the right actions—and reactions.

PMA is the one stabilizer that you and I need to meet any of life's storms. On a ship, a stabilizer is a kind of shock absorber, a kind of gyroscope that keeps vessels steady in the heavy seas. I remember one trip on a rough sea, but because of the ship's stabilizer, the trip was most pleasant and in no way uncomfortable. On a similar trip, many years ago, the ship had no stabilizer and it was rough, truly rough. But any stabilizer, be it a gyroscope or otherwise, is useless if it isn't used.

And so it is with PMA. It must be developed and used. People who do not develop a positive mental attitude toward life and work become unhappy. Some even develop psychosomatic illnesses, or have nervous breakdowns because they are overwhelmed by any turbulence in their lives. In addition, each of them brings misery to their associates and loved ones.

By developing positive thoughts and eliminating negative thoughts, you use an effective, natural stabilizer that is far superior to any mechanical gyroscope. You have the power to direct your thoughts, control your emotions, and thus ordain your destiny.

How to Do It: PMA the Ten-Step Way

What you will learn here is a simple, ten-step formula for developing and maintaining a Positive Mental Attitude. The ten steps will not simply teach you PMA, they will encourage you to put it into practice, and by doing so, make it a part of your life. A Chinese proverb concerning learning says: "I hear and I forget. I see and I remember. I do and I understand."

The ten steps to developing and maintaining PMA require more than your hearing and seeing—they require your action! If you do what is outlined here, PMA will be yours. The ten steps are intricately interwoven, and each step strengthens the others. Just think, all English literature is composed of only twenty-six letters. All music is composed from only twelve notes, all colors from only three primary colors. Just think! So much from so little. If one letter is eliminated in writing, what happens? What if, for example, you eliminated the vowel "a" from this book? If just one note is eliminated throughout a concerto, instead of harmony you have discord. If one of the three primary colors of red, blue, or yellow is missing, you won't have the colors you are seeking. If you have all the numbers to a combination safe but one, you don't enter the safe. It is imperative that you learn and use all ten steps toward PMA.

These ten steps are the heart of the matter—they are

your "learn-by-doing" keys. Each step includes a LEARN BY DOING suggestion that will help you to incorporate that particular step into your mental makeup. Each step also includes a short SELF-TEST. There is no scoring of these tests; instead they are designed to provoke you into examining the ways you are thinking about PMA, and to expand your ideas about all the ways it can be applied in your life. At the end of each step, you'll also find WORDS FROM THE WISE, inspiring comments from others who have learned PMA's value. A special bonus tip will then show you something concrete you can do to help make PMA work.

How you use the ten-step way to PMA is up to you, of course, but here is one method you might follow:

1. Initially read all ten steps.
2. Concentrate on one step each day, for ten days, assimilating it into the very substance of your routine.
3. Repeat the cycle. Repetition is an important aspect of learning, so you might choose to cycle through the ten steps again and again until you know and apply them intimately and from memory.

Another possibility would be to take a week with each step, making its practice part of all your affairs. At the end of ten weeks, you will be well on your way as a Positive Mental Attitude graduate student, an expert in its application to yourself and to every person, circumstance, and event that comes your way.

Fringe Benefits of PMA

With the promise that PMA will be yours comes another—the promise that this formula will help you discover an entirely new, wonderful person who now lies dormant within you. You will discover a new, happy, exciting self. By following this formula, you can acquire and keep a joyous and positive attitude at all times throughout your life, even when you encounter problems or difficulties. W. Clement Stone says, "Whenever I have a problem or difficulty in business or any other problem, I say, 'That's good,' and then I say, 'Now, what's so good about it?' and then I find out how I can turn these disadvantages into advantages."

And if anyone has a real problem, they're very, very fortunate. That is, they're fortunate if they adopt a PMA philosophy. With PMA, if you have problems, you recognize these problems may be blessings in disguise. You will know there is no one who is truly successful who cannot look back and see a period in his life where he had a very serious problem and solved it intelligently. Of course, if you have a serious problem, at the moment you may think you're very unfortunate. But one of the best self-motivators—one that I heartily recommend—is "With every adversity, there is a seed of an equivalent or greater benefit." Put another way, "With every disadvantage, there is an advantage."

You can experience the enthusiasm and thrill of seeing PMA help you get any worthy thing in life you desire. It requires only your commitment to making PMA work for you, and no matter how strange a way of thinking it may seem to you at first, the more you put it into practice, the more you will reap its many rewards.

Why not begin now?

2

Step One: Take Possession of Your Own Mind with Conviction

There is only one pathway to a PMA: you must take control of your own mind with *conviction*. Your mind is one of the great marvels of the universe. Astronomer, mathematician, and physicist Freeman Dyson says about the mind:

> It is remarkable that mind enters our awareness of nature on two separate levels. At the highest level, the level of human consciousness, our minds are somehow directly aware of the complicated flow of electrical and chemical patterns in our brains. At the lowest level, the level of single atoms and electrons, the mind of an observer is again involved in the description of events. Between lies the level . . . where mechanical models are adequate and the mind

appears to be irrelevant. But I, as a physicist, cannot help suspecting that there is a logical connection between the two ways in which the mind appears in my universe.

. . . I do not feel like an alien in this universe. The more I examine the universe and study the details of its architecture, the more evidence I find that the universe in some sense must have known that we were coming.

Dyson believes that the mind permeates the universe, showing up at both the level of the least of things and the most of things, in the activity of electrons and the activity of humans. Where the universe and your mind come together, where the least of things connects with the greatest of things, is the point at which you can exercise control of your life and the world around you.

Remember W. Clement Stone's observation: you are a mind with a body. You can direct your thoughts, control your emotions, and ordain your destiny. William James certainly appreciated the pent-up power that every person possesses. I remind you of his conviction: "We become what we think about most of the time."

Everyone has the same wondrous treasure—a brain and a nervous system. Each person who is "normal" (in the broadest sense of the word) has inherited the power to achieve in principle anything in life anyone else has achieved or is now achieving. Your passions, emotions, instincts, tendencies, feelings, moods, attitudes, and habits are all yours to direct to such an end. How you use them is up to you. As with all natural powers, each of these latent abilities has the potential for good, but the use one puts each to can be positive, neutral, or negative.

At birth these powers are latent. They are like new tools in a hardware store—polished and gleaming, ready to be used, but incapable of acting alone. They require a user. As the newborn baby develops into adulthood, the evidence of these functions of the mind becomes apparent in thoughts and actions. From time to time, because of ignorance, fear, or some other unfortunate influence, many of them go unused and become dormant.

But no matter what you have done so far in your life, you still have the power and ability to use the tools of your mind effectively and efficiently. You can direct, control, neutralize, and harmonize them—all by developing a Positive Mental Attitude.

Your mind has ten billion cells—give or take a few—which is twice as many as there are people in the world. These cells are all interconnected, and every one of them is meant to be your servant. Yet the most intelligent of people come nowhere near fully utilizing the available power. Many of the most important people in history had an IQ of no higher than average. Their achievements and greatness were due to their ability to use and direct their mental powers. They had superior PMA quotients! You have unlimited mental capacities, but it is up to you to use this power of your mind to think positively, so that they all work to your advantage.

LEARN BY DOING
Take Possession of Your Own Mind with Conviction

Note: This is the first of the practical exercises provided for you. Take the time, make the time, time and again, to do the exercises for all ten steps.

Make a copy of the following "creed" and put it somewhere you will be sure to see it first thing in the morning; perhaps the bathroom mirror might be the place, or in your dresser drawer. Don't wait to say it until you believe it—saying it will help you believe it.

I BELIEVE MY MIND IS MY OWN.

I BELIEVE I CAN TAKE POSSESSION OF MY OWN MIND.

I BELIEVE I CAN DIRECT AND CONTROL MY EMOTIONS, MOODS, FEELINGS, INTELLECT, TENDENCIES, ATTITUDES, PASSIONS, AND HABITS WITH THE INTENTION OF DEVELOPING A POSITIVE MENTAL ATTITUDE.

I WILL DEVELOP A POSITIVE MENTAL ATTITUDE.

The Winner's Commitment

The America's Cup is the most prestigious sailing trophy in the world. It's called the America's Cup because for 138 years, it was won by teams from the United States. Then, in 1983, the Australians stunned the world by winning the cup.

Dennis Conner was captain of the American yacht that lost that year. But four years later, he and his crew aboard *Stars & Stripes* brought the America's Cup back to the U.S. To do that Conner had to overcome incredible odds, including the perception that he was the man who had lost the America's Cup in the first place.

At the core of Conner's achievement was what he calls "the commitment to the commitment," the dedication to his goal that allowed him to focus all his energies on building the kind of boat and assembling the kind of crew that could win. "Once you make the commitment . . . ," Conner says, "you become focused on one act. There is a new Main Event in center ring, and all the other 'acts' in your life have to take place somewhere else."

Make your commitment to your commitment to developing PMA today.

SELF-TEST

❧

Answer the following questions honestly:

1. You're about to meet with your boss about your raise. How do you spend the half hour beforehand?

a) Talking with coworkers to keep your mind off the big event.

b) Mentally rehearsing your challenges and hints that you're ready to quit if you don't get the salary increase you want.

c) Reviewing the accomplishments you've made in the past year, the ways they have benefited the organization, and your plans for building on them in the coming year.

2. Your daughter has brought home a report card that says she is having trouble in a subject at school. How do you react?

a) Tell her, "I had the same problem, and I did all right. Don't worry about it."

b) Tell her that she must spend an extra hour each evening working on the subject, and that until her grades come up she cannot be involved in any extracurricular activities.

c) Tell her that it's good to know about her difficulties

early before they become big. Offer to go over her homework with her after she does it because you know that even if the subject is a tough one, she *can* understand it with some extra effort.

3. Your next-door neighbor has a new puppy that loves to dig up your lawn. How do you respond?

a) Grimace and say, "Isn't that adorable?"
b) Threaten to call the dogcatcher if you ever see the puppy in your yard again.
c) Tell your neighbor what is happening, suggest that this is a habit that should be stopped before the puppy causes real trouble, and ask what you can do to help.

4. Your business is just getting off the ground when a competitor starts undercutting your prices. What do you do?

a) Decide to tough it out.
b) Tell all your customers that the competition cuts corners and will raise prices just as soon as you've been driven out of business.
c) Keep your prices the same but offer better service than your competitor while doubling your efforts to let your customers know how much you value their business.

In each of the above situations, an "a" answer represents an attempt to ignore a potential problem or opportunity. It is not a PMA response because it means you accept a situation as something over which you have no influence. Having PMA means that you recognize that your response to a situation, good or bad, is one of the most powerful means you have of achieving success.

A "b" response is the opposite of PMA. In each of them you are concentrating on the negative aspects of the situation, mentally preparing yourself for conflict and trouble. You are also usually telling other people that you expect them to give you that conflict and trouble. A PMA response does not ignore what is wrong in a given situation, but it realizes that the best way out is to look for solutions, not more problems.

A "c" response is a PMA response. It mentally prepares you for things to go your way, and it tells other people that you know this will happen as well. It is not a response that ignores trouble; it is a response that cuts trouble off at the pass. This will require action on your part, usually immediate, but in the long run it will take less effort than if you made the problem worse by ignoring it or escalating tensions.

Bonus: During the day, when circumstances, people, or situations threaten your Positive Mental Attitude resolution, use this quick sentence to get you back on track:

MY MIND IS MY OWN.
I WILL CONTROL IT!

❧ Words from the Wise ❧

"Whatsoever thy hand findeth to do, do it with all thy might."—Ecclesiastes 9:10

"If you are distressed by anything external, the pain is not due to the thing itself, but to your estimate of it; and this you have the power to revoke at any moment."—Marcus Aurelius

"Whatever you do, or dream you can, begin it. Boldness has genius, power, and magic in it."
　　　　　　　　　　　　　　—Johann Goethe

"Circumstances—what are circumstances? I make circumstances."—Napoleon

"Men are born to succeed, not to fail."
　　　　　　　　　　　—Henry David Thoreau

"Always bear in mind that your own resolution to success is more important than any other one thing."—Abraham Lincoln

"Destiny is not a matter of chance; it is a matter of choice. It is not a thing to be waited for; it is a thing to be achieved."—William Jennings Bryan

"It's a funny thing about life; if you refuse to accept anything but the best, you very often get it."
                                    —W. Somerset Maugham

"In the last analysis our only freedom is the freedom to discipline ourselves."—Bernard Baruch

"The future belongs to those who believe in the beauty of their dreams."—Eleanor Roosevelt

3

Step Two: Keep Your Mind on the Things You Want and off the Things You Don't Want

◦∾◦

Once you take possession of your own mind, you have to keep control of it, and the best way is to keep it focused on the things you want and off the things you don't want.

"A picture is worth a thousand words," the old saying goes. Much of how you think takes place in words, yet the most profoundly motivational thinking you do takes place in pictures, not words. If an idea occurs to you, it's usually in the form of a picture of something happening, rather than as a sentence that runs through your head. Pictures are an immediate and powerful way of thinking.

Your mind's image-making ability takes place at a far older, deeper level than its language-making. Human language-making developed relatively recently. Pictures and images have a direct, basic, elemental appeal to your emotions and feelings, while words have only an indirect appeal. Words must first be translated into pictures before the deepest levels of your mind will accept them and be changed by them.

You must learn, therefore, to discipline your thoughts and visualize the things you want, the wholesome characteristics you wish to acquire. Suppose, for example, that forcefulness was a characteristic you felt a need for. Do not content yourself with *saying*, "I must be more forceful." Rather, imagine how you would look if you were more forceful. What would be the expression on your face? What would be the attitude of your body?

You can train yourself to act and react with good, wholesome, honest, and healthy visual images to any situation, person, or circumstance you encounter. By visualizing the good in another person in real, tangible ways, you can guarantee that you will experience it. By envisioning (in your mind's eye) the positive outcome of a situation, you can move it along toward reality.

Recognize this truth: with every adversity, failure, defeat, sorrow, or unpleasant circumstance (either of your own or someone else's making), you have the opportunity to react positively. Seek and ye shall find. You can recognize the seed of an equivalent or greater benefit, a seed that will grow into the actual greater benefit or blessing—if helped along by your visualization of its happening.

One way to aid the developing of a Positive Mental Attitude in the face of adversity is to realize what is done is done. You cannot change the past but you can affect what happens in the present and the future. Say to yourself, "Whatever happened, happened for the best, and that's good!" Then set to work to figure out what good can result from the experience.

In Every Adversity . . .

It can be hard to believe at times that underneath bad news is good news, but many of today's most successful people have learned this lesson very well.

- Chuck Yeager was a fighter pilot over occupied France in World War II when his plane was shot down. He single-handedly escaped German patrols and dragged his navigator over the mountains to Spain, where they finally found safety. The Army Air Corps was ready to send him home after that, but Yeager refused to go. "Without realizing it," he says, "I was about to take charge of my life. If I had submitted to being sent home, I doubt whether the Army Air Corps would have been interested in retaining my services after the war ended." Instead, Yeager became the first pilot to fly faster than the speed of sound.
- Terrie Williams was a social worker in a hospital who loved working with people, but found herself overwhelmed by their problems and ready to quit. She realized that what she loved was sharing *good* news, not bad, and started a publicity company that soon lined up clients like Miles Davis, Eddie Murphy, and Jackie Joyner-Kersee. She never would have become one of the country's best publicists if she hadn't faced the disappointment of seeing her first ambition fall apart.

Close your mental doors behind you on unpleasant circumstances or failures you have experienced in the past. Dwelling on failures, letdowns, or negative feelings about others can only make situations worse. Learn to let your dissatisfaction with anything inspire you.

Inspirational dissatisfaction is that divine discontent that throughout the history of man has produced all real progress and reform.

Inspirational dissatisfaction is conducive to self-inspiration to action. It motivates you to learn from defeat, to turn disadvantages into advantages, and to work harder to reach your goals regardless of the obstacles you meet.

Take, for example, the true case history of the boy who almost flunked in every grade in grammar school. As a teenager he was lucky to be passed through high school. Then, as a freshman at the state university, he flunked out in the very first semester. Now that was good, for then something happened to develop inspirational dissatisfaction within him.

He knew he had the ability to succeed, and on reflection, he realized that it was necessary to work hard to make up for lost time. With this new positive mental attitude, he entered a junior college. He worked hard. He kept trying, and on graduation day, he received the honor of being second highest in his class.

No, he didn't stop there. He applied for admission to one of the nation's leading universities where scholastic standards are exceedingly high and admission is most difficult to obtain. Because of his positive mental attitude and his record of achievement in junior college, he was admitted. And there too he developed an enviable record as an outstanding student—for every adversity carries with it a seed of an equivalent or greater benefit.

Keep your mind focused on the things you want to achieve or stand for in life. Use your brain for controlled, optimistic thinking. Take possession of your mind and direct it to images of your choosing. Do not let circumstances or people dictate negative visual images.

Remember: Yesterday is gone forever. Tomorrow may never come. Only today is yours to live in.

LEARN BY DOING
Keep Your Mind on the Things You Want and off the Things You Don't Want

Thinking in visual terms rather than words is sometimes difficult. This exercise will help you begin the training to form and keep visual images:

Make a list of three things you want. One should be a wholesome characteristic you wish to acquire. One should be an improved relationship with someone close to you. And one should be some material possession you would like to have. Be specific!

Characteristic:_____

Relationship:_____

Possession:_____

Consider each of these. Think of a way to show them visually. Look through old magazines or newspapers for pictures that will symbolize for you the mental image you have made.

Use your own richly creative imagination to complete this exercise. The following suggestions are just meant as primers. Suppose "generosity" was the characteristic you chose, for example. Then you might look for a picture of someone with an open, outstretched hand. If you want to improve some special relationship with "more quality time together," you might look for a picture of a clock. And if the personal possession you wanted was a Mercedes Benz, look for an ad featuring that car and cut out the picture of it.

Put these pictures where you will see them every day. Use them as visual cues to help your mind form the mental image of the characteristic, the improved relationship, and the possession. And then believe that you're going to get what you want!

SELF-TEST

Answer the following questions honestly:

1. Your job as a sales rep takes you into a territory where all your customers had a bad experience with your predecessor and are reluctant to do business with your company. How do you respond?

   a) Act as if nothing was wrong before.
   b) Find out specifically what went wrong for each customer, then write a detailed report to your supervisor about all the problems you have been saddled with so that it is clear you have been placed in a bad situation.
   c) Find out specifically what went wrong for each customer, then use this knowledge to make sure that things flow smoothly and that your customers know you're dedicated to keeping it that way.

2. Your son has an accident with the car that will cost thousands of dollars to repair. How do you react?

   a) Sigh, "Teenagers. Thank goodness for insurance."
   b) Forbid him to drive again, and tell him that for his irresponsibility he is grounded for the next six months.
   c) Tell him that it is his responsibility to get a job to pay for the repairs, and that as soon as he has done so, he can use the car again.

3. You are involved in a civic organization that is trying to raise money for a local charity by sponsoring a flea market. Two weeks before the event, you have had few donations of merchandise. What do you do?

a) Hope for the best.

b) Call the charity and tell them not to expect much money. Call the other members of the organization and predict disappointment so they get used to the idea.

c) Call your list of potential donors and remind them that they will be doing great things for the community. Ask if you can make things easier by picking up donations, and when you can drop by to do so.

4. Your doctor tells you that you have borderline high blood pressure. You can begin to take medication for it, or you can make changes in your lifestyle that should bring it down. How do you respond?

a) Ignore his advice.

b) Take the medication, since all that advice about what to eat and do changes all the time anyway, and you hate being on some kind of program and know that you would never stick with it.

c) Start exercising, begin eating more healthy foods, and use meditation and visualization to decrease stress in your life and concentrate on being a healthier, less stressed person.

Once again, "a" responses represent bad moves. They all allow you to *pretend* that there is no issue to be dealt with, even though you know there is. You may tell your-self that there is no problem, but it *is* there and when it gets even bigger you will be completely unprepared to deal with it. PMA does not ignore a situation. With PMA you concentrate on good results that you know are pos-sible because you are making them happen.

A "b" response demonstrates doing just the opposite. You tell yourself and everyone else that a negative out-come is certain, and you resign yourself to it. You do not act, and you reinforce your inaction by telling yourself that it would be worthless to act anyway. PMA always requires that you be active in a situation, and the first place to begin is with your own attitude.

If you are acting with PMA, you would have chosen "c" answers. Concentrating on making a bad situation good does not mean shying away from admitting there is a problem. In each of the examples, you must acknow-ledge the problem to begin to correct it. But the key is expressing to yourself and often to others that you be-lieve that a solution can be found. These solutions are often greater in their scope than the initial problem.

For instance, in the first example, by showing your customers that you are dedicated to serving them well, you not only overcome their dislike of your predecessor, you make yourself valuable to them, and thus to your company. In the second example, by giving your son an opportunity to make amends, you teach him a lesson about responsibility and work, and show him that if he makes a mistake, he can overcome it—a good example of a PMA lesson shared.

In question three, you concentrate on the benefit of

the project, and you draw others into creating that benefit. People like to be given the opportunity to help others,
and not only will they respect you for making it possible
for them, they will see that you are an action-oriented
person. And in question four, by taking responsibility
for your health you are addressing the causes of your
problem, not simply papering them over. Even if the
steps you take prove insufficient to avoid the need for
medication, you have still improved your situation.

PMA focuses your mind on positive solutions, and
when you train yourself to find them, doing so becomes
a valuable habit.

Bonus: Using the power of visualization to keep your
mind off what you don't want is just as easy. Earlier I
said, "Close your mental doors behind you on unpleasant circumstances or failures you have experienced in
the past." Use this as a visual trigger to form an image.
Imagine yourself in a long corridor in the midst of your
brain. Opening onto this hallway are many doors, and
one of them is labeled DEFEATS AND FAILURES. Now
picture yourself walking purposefully toward that door
while taking a huge key out of your pocket. Firmly and
decisively close that door and lock it. Pocket the key
with a smile. Any time you feel the shadow of old negative thoughts stealing upon you, say to yourself:

I HAVE THE KEY IN MY POCKET.

I HAVE LOCKED THAT THOUGHT UP.

And smile because you know it's true.

❧ Words from the Wise ❧

"He did it with all his heart, and prospered."
—2 Chronicles 31:21

"Let us go singing as far as we go; the road will be less tedious."—Virgil

"This one thing I do, forgetting those things which are behind, and reaching forth unto those things which are before."—Philippians 3:13

"Our doubts are traitors, and make us lose the good we might oft win by fearing to attempt."
—William Shakespeare

"Never despair, but if you do, work on in despair."
—Edmund Burke

"The thing always happens that you really believe in, and the belief in a thing makes it happen."
—Frank Lloyd Wright

"To be happy, drop the words 'if only' and substitute instead the words 'next time.' "—Smiley Blanton

"Once a decision was made I did not worry about it afterward."—Harry S. Truman

"Act as if it were impossible to fail."
—Dorothea Brande

"Losers visualize the penalties of failures. Winners visualize the rewards of success."—Rob Gilbert

4

Step Three: Live the Golden Rule

Do unto others as you would have them do unto you. Conversely, do not do unto others what you would not have them do unto you.

This familiar and seemingly simple step has tremendous merit. Sometimes living the Golden Rule means you must stand up for others, be their guardian, protector, and advocate. Martin Niemoller, a Protestant leader of resistance to Nazi tyranny, knew that truth. Speaking to postwar audiences, Niemoller would say:

> The Nazis came for the Communists and I didn't speak up because I was not a Communist. Then they came for the Jews and I did not speak up because I was not a Jew. Then they came for the trade unionists and I didn't speak up because I was not a trade unionist. Then they came for the Catholics and I

was a Protestant. So I didn't speak up. Then they came for me . . . by that time there was no one to speak up for anyone.

Yes, do unto others as you would have them do unto you. Consistently look for the good in everyone and in every circumstance. In dealings with your family, friends, and business associates, be a good-finder, not a fault-finder. Give help, praise, and encouragement instead of criticism, blame, or revenge. Walk the extra mile to help someone.

The PMA concept is that the little difference that makes the big difference as to whether a person is happy, unhappy, or miserable is whether his attitude toward himself and others is positive or negative.

For example, the surest way to find happiness for yourself is to devote your thoughts, energies, and activities toward making others happy in little things daily. You can make yourself unhappy or miserable by thinking only in terms of yourself and not the reactions of others to what you do, or don't do, say or don't say.

Lloyd C. Douglas's book *The Magnificent Obsession* points out that when you bring happiness to someone else, it will return to you many times over if you do it without boastfulness or looking for personal rewards.

"Big Jim" Daniell knows the power of being happy. Before he arrived in 1976 at RMI, a producer of titanium, the company was in deep trouble. Since then, as the new president, Mr. Daniell has turned things around. How did he do it? Not with computers, not with consultants, not with MBAs—but with a Positive Mental Attitude.

Big Jim learned the names of all seven hundred employees at RMI. "When you meet a man without a smile, give him one of yours," reads the sign hanging on the wall. Big Jim is giving out smiles all the time as he cruises the plant floor in his electric cart, joking with workers. "Believe it or not, for a big, dumb football player"—he was captain of the Cleveland Browns in 1945—"I have a philosophy: do unto others as you would have them do unto you," he says.

Mr. Daniell's philosophy works. RMI's sales are up. Productivity is up. Morale is up, and Mr. Daniell is a happy man.

Share a portion of what you have. In sharing with others, you give away a portion of yourself—but that which remains with you multiplies and grows. At the same time, you are challenging others to a higher, more creative way of life. By helping others, you have in turn helped yourself, and together you have set in motion a chain reaction of goodwill and PMA.

LEARN BY DOING
Live the Golden Rule

Think of three things you would like people to do for you.

1._____

2._____

3._____

Now turn them around. How can you do each of them for another? Use Step #2 as an aid in this: form an image of what you actually see happening in your mind's eye. If it will help, find a symbolic picture that will help you visualize what you are going to do.

Now go and do it!

When You Get a Little, Give a Little

Time and again, successful people have shared their success with other individuals and their communities. It wins them respect, cooperation, and personal satisfaction.

- Terry Evenson was very successful in a series of business ventures. One way he shared his success was by starting a scholarship program for bright but poor students. Now that these people have had the opportunity to make successes of themselves, they in turn are helping to fund scholarships for other students, all in the belief that giving someone a chance to succeed is important.
- Bill Cosby is one of the most powerful and popular entertainers in the world. He makes it his business to meet with other aspiring entertainers and give them career advice and encouragement that he knows they will need as they struggle to build a career.

SELF-TEST

❧

Consider the following questions:

1. Three days ago you gave your associate all the data you had collected and analyzed for an important report due tomorrow. Today you learn that he has made little progress in preparing it. How do you respond?

a) Say nothing, so as to avoid putting any pressure on him.

b) Prepare a memo to him and your boss outlining the fact that you fulfilled your responsibilities on time and making it clear that any failure to have the report ready does not lie on your shoulders.

c) Offer to help complete the report.

2. Your in-laws are getting older and are not able to do all the tasks they once did. How do you respond?

a) Stay out of it, since it is none of your business. Nobody likes nosy in-laws.

b) Insist that it is time for them to move into a retirement home before they become a burden.

c) Offer to run errands for them and help out around the house and yard twice a month while recruiting other family members as well.

3. You're driving on a crowded freeway at high speeds and another car is tailgating you very closely. How do you react?

    a) Continue driving as you were.

    b) Flash your brakes and slow down. Do your best to teach the other driver to show a little courtesy on the road.

    c) Move aside and let the other car pass.

4. At the service station you've patronized for years, a new mechanic is rude to you and treats you as if you know nothing. How do you respond?

    a) Put up with it and assume that he will eventually be fired.

    b) Take your business elsewhere.

    c) Speak to the manager privately and explain you were surprised by the way you were treated, since you have always been happy there.

You know by now that an "a" response is a passive one that defies the action required of a positive mental attitude. PMA identifies problems and works to correct them; by ignoring these situations, you let them fester until they become something larger and potentially more troublesome. Sometimes it may seem that staying above the fray is the least complicated approach, but it can easily let a situation get out of hand. You may find others wondering why you are so passive in a situation when instead you can be displaying leadership and judgment.

The "b" responses are active, but they almost always

heighten tension and prepare other people to think of you as an opponent or a whiner. When problems arise, people look for someone with the initiative to seek a solution, not someone who exacerbates tension or stomps off in a huff. Why should anyone choose to deal with you when your attitude is always to lay blame elsewhere or avoid responsibility? If, as in the example on the freeway, you are dealing with someone who is already displaying poor judgment, it can be impossible to predict what your provocation may bring, and the consequences can quickly escalate beyond your ability to cope. Instead of issuing challenges, offer understanding. Your actions should reflect the way you hope others will deal with you.

A "c" response encourages others to think of you as someone who has always been willing to cooperate, to lend a hand, to do something out of the ordinary. Sometimes this will involve people you interact with all the time, people whose help and willing cooperation you may suddenly depend upon, whether they are coworkers with expertise to lend, in-laws whom you may turn to in times of need, or a service station owner who gets your car running again the day before a big vacation.

Sometimes you will find that the PMA you display in living by the Golden Rule is directed at someone you have never met before and will never see again. You might never see a direct benefit from your actions. But others will, beginning with the people you respond positively to, and continuing with those they respond positively to in turn. By acting with PMA, you add to the general supply of PMA in the entire world, improving every community you work and live in. If you've ever been amazed at the ability of someone you know to get help at the most unlikely times, odds are that person has been living life with PMA. As the Scriptures say, "As ye sow, so shall ye also reap."

Bonus: Think of three things you don't want people to do to you.

1._____
2._____
3._____

Now turn them around. Here's how:

Be generous. When you share with others a part of what you have, that which remains multiplies and grows. Examples:

- Give a smile to everyone you meet. Smile with your eyes and you'll smile and receive smiles.
- Give a kind word with a kindly thought behind the word—you will be kind and receive kind words.
- Give appreciation—warmth from the heart. You will appreciate and be appreciated.
- Give honor, credit, and applause, the victor's wreath. You will be honored and receive credit and applause.
- Give time for a worthy cause with eagerness. You will be worthy and richly rewarded.
- Give hope—the magic ingredient for success. You will have hope and be made hopeful.

- Give happiness—a most treasured state of mind. You will have courage and be encouraged.
- Give cheer—the verbal sunshine. You will be cheerful and cheered.
- Give a pleasant response—the neutralizer of irritants. You will be pleasant and receive pleasant responses.

❧ Words from the Wise ❧

"Hatred stirreth up strifes: but love covereth all sins."—Proverbs 10:12

"What you do not want done to yourself, do not do to others."—Confucius

"We secure our friends not by accepting favors but by doing them."—Thucydides

"Teach me my God and King, in all things thee to see, and what I do in any thing, to do it as for thee."—George Herbert

"Example is not the main thing in influencing others. It is the only thing."—Albert Schweitzer

"Too many people do not care what happens as long as it does not happen to them."
—William Howard Taft

5

Step Four: Eliminate All Negative Thoughts by Self-Inspection

❧

Most people do not realize that they are thinking negatively unless they make a conscious effort to inspect their thoughts, actions, and reactions. The process of self-analysis is simple. Just ask yourself, "Is this positive or negative?" When you fail to take possession of your own mind and direct it to your own choosing by employing the power of visualization, the chances are good your reactions will be negative instead of positive.

Notice how living the Golden Rule is a positive aid to you. Clearly, if you are concerned with doing good to others, and avoiding bad, there is little room for negative thoughts to operate.

Especially as you are beginning the exciting process of developing a Positive Mental Attitude, however, old habits will assert themselves from time to time. You will find negative thoughts lurking about, ready to slip out the moment you open that door a crack. The following four reasons probably cover most of the times that negative thoughts occur to you.

1. You are feeling sorry for yourself and are indulging in self-pity.
2. You are passing judgment or blaming a person, situation, or environment. (Alcoholics talk about "taking the geographic cure," meaning trying to solve their drinking problem by blaming it on where they live.)
3. Your ego has been hurt or deflated. Your pride has been damaged.
4. The most obvious one, but the one most people find hardest to recognize, is that you are being self-ish about yourself, someone, or something.

The more you practice PMA, the more you will be able to recognize negative thoughts as soon as they occur. But as you begin the great process of incorporating PMA into your life, you will have to rely on more conscious analysis. In most cases, negative thoughts will still be easy to spot because they lead you to consider violating the Golden Rule with regard to others, or because you will tell yourself something about yourself that you would regard as an insult from another person.

If the thought flashes into your mind that you cannot do something, ask yourself what you would think if a stranger on the street walked up and said the same thing to you. Treat such thoughts just as you would such a

Who's Really Being Selfish?

Dr. Bertice Berry is a successful stand-up comic, actress, and singer who had her own television talk show and performs and lectures all over the country. She was the first member of her family ever to go to college, so when she graduated, she expected all her relations to show up and cheer.

When she found out none of her family members was coming, she was furious, and decided to skip the graduation ceremonies until a professor told her she was just being selfish. She did go, and she was stunned when the university gave her its most outstanding student award, which was presented by a two-time Nobel prize winner.

She almost missed an incredible honor, all because her pride was wounded. Instead, she overcame it and moved steadily up the ladder of success.

stranger. Say, "You know nothing about what I am capable of doing. You are way out of line to say anything like that."

The negative thoughts that appear in your mind are the product of a past you have decided to put behind you. They come from experiences you have decided to overcome, and they have nothing to do with the kind of thinker and doer you are making yourself into. Counter them with an immediate and forceful antidote in the form of a concrete positive thought about yourself or the person or circumstance involved.

LEARN BY DOING
Eliminate All Negative Thoughts by Self-Inspection

Make a checklist to carry in your pocket or wallet. Call it: "Parties I Refuse to Attend":

1. Pity party—You're feeling sorry for yourself.
2. Patsy party—You're looking for someone to blame.
3. Pride party—You're suffering from injured ego.
4. Pig party—You're being selfish.

Review this list at the beginning of your day. When negative thoughts surface, take a private moment to ask yourself, "What's going on?" Look at your list of no-thank-you parties and see if one of those causes is at work. Then banish it.

SELF-TEST

Answer the following questions honestly:

1. Your bid to work for a prestigious and lucrative client is turned down and the project goes to a rival group. What flashes through your head?

  a) "It just wasn't meant to be."
  b) "I would have won the job if the other firm wasn't so desperate to undercut me. They took the job at a loss just to keep me from getting the work."
  c) "I need to find out what made them go with the other company. This is a chance to identify problem areas and correct them."

2. Your daughter drops out of college to work in a restaurant kitchen. What occurs to you?

  a) "She has never had very much drive."
  b) "She's rebelling and is trying to embarrass me after all the money I spent sending her to college."
  c) "She must not have been happy in college and I should find out why."

3. You run for election as president of your local community association and are defeated. What thoughts do you have?

a) "Another lesson learned. I should stop trying to win popularity contests."

b) "If these people can't see what a good president I'd be, then I shouldn't be wasting my time with them."

c) "My opponent knows some things I don't about exciting people's interests. This is someone to learn from. I bet we could make a great team working together."

4. You know you should lose fifteen pounds, but try as you might, so far you haven't been successful. What attitude do you take?

a) "Hey, I could be worse off. At least I haven't gained anything."

b) "I'm paying too much attention to this fitness craze. I'm never going to lose that weight and I ought to stop torturing myself."

c) "I need to find a new approach that I can stay interested in so that I can improve my health."

There is an approach to life known as "go with the flow," that sometimes seems very appealing, since it appears to eliminate worry and stress. But it is often a cover for sending yourself a series of negative messages about who you are and what you can do. The "a" responses above reflect this. They often incorporate a good amount of subtle self-pity, along the lines of "I just wasn't born to be a natural leader or athlete," or "Life has saddled me with many burdens and the best I can do is shuffle on."

A Positive Mental Attitude doesn't let you get away with this kind of thinking. The idea may pop into your head, but you consider it and realize that it is a way of avoiding action and responsibility. When this happens, you can reject the thought and counter it with positive suggestion; the more often you do this consciously, the more often it will happen reflexively, until the negative thoughts simply stop coming.

Instead of blaming circumstance, it is also easy to blame others because they seem to offer the easiest targets for your self-pity and wounded pride. This is exemplified by the "b" responses. Of course, taking such an approach never leads to action to resolve the situation, and can easily make matters much worse. You must accurately identify the source of adversity to find the hidden benefit inside, and if you ignore this truth, all your troubles will be for nothing.

The "c" responses above exemplify exactly this approach. They acknowledge that a problem exists and set about to find out more about it in the conviction that something can be done. This discovery process will often require you to rely once again on your PMA, because you may learn things you never expected about yourself or your situation. But if you respond to such revelations with the attitude that what you have learned is important and that you will be able to deal with it, you will have reaped one of the greatest benefits of PMA—increased self-understanding and self-confidence.

Bonus: "Banishing" a negative thought is easier than you may think. Remember your step #2 Bonus Idea? YOU

HAVE THE KEY. Lock that negative thought up where it belongs, in the dungeon! A Positive Mental Attitude puts the power to do that in your hands as well as in your head.

∾ Words from the Wise ∾

"I am fearfully and wonderfully made."
— Psalms 139:14

"Self-trust is the first secret of success."
— Ralph Waldo Emerson

"Tell yourself in your secret reveries, I was made to handle affairs." — Andrew Carnegie

"Rancor is an outpouring of a feeling of inferiority." — José Ortega y Gasset

"Discouragement is simply the despair of wounded self-love." — François de Fénelon

"Never build a case against yourself."
— Robert Rowbottom

"A man can lose sight of everything when he's bent on revenge, and it ain't worth it." — Louis L'Amour

"You gain strength, courage, and confidence by every experience in which you really stop to look fear in the face. You are able to say to yourself, 'I lived through this horror. I can take the next thing that comes along.' You must do the thing you think you cannot do." — Eleanor Roosevelt

6

Step Five: Be Happy! Make Others Happy!

To be happy, ACT happy! Just as you can think your way into a new way of acting, so you can act your way into a new thinking. Be enthusiastic. To be enthusiastic, act enthusiastic. Smile at yourself, and at the world.

You will eventually experience a feeling of inner joy and enthusiasm that will show itself without your having to concentrate on it. People recognize positive people (and they want to be around them). This change in the quality of your life happens when you eliminate negative thoughts and keep your mind on good, wholesome, constructive thoughts, memories, and experiences. And it is easy to maintain a joyous attitude, because it is just as easy to think positively as it is to think negatively.

If you have to worry, worry positively. In his best-selling *Psycho-Cybernetics*, Dr. Maxwell Maltz tells readers to "worry constructively." He says that worrying is thinking about what could go wrong, and that the antidote to this affliction is to consciously dwell on what could go right.

Here are two simple rules to follow for constructive worrying. Write them down on an index card and carry the card in your pocket as your "prescription" for worrying:

1. The best outcome that could happen to my challenge of _____ might be _____.

2. This could happen. After all, it's very possible that _____ could indeed happen.

Periodically ingest a dose of optimism with these rules. Imagine what the desired outcome to your problem would be like. Then play back these thoughts in your mind, gradually internalizing feelings of confidence and courage.

Maltz believes that the subconscious mind can't distinguish between a real experience and an imaginary one. To capitalize on this theory, he suggests the following exercise: establish a designated period each day when you can close your eyes and daydream about your goals. Picture yourself as having already achieved these objectives. Imagine what your attained goal feels, smells, and looks like. When you do find yourself dwelling on negative thoughts, immediately command yourself to stop. Then replace those dismal images with mental pictures of what you really want to happen in your life. Try it. It works!

The wonderful feeling that you will experience is PMA.

LEARN BY DOING
Chronicle Your Success

It is important to examine your accomplishments and successes. Reduce to a formula, in writing, the details of the experiences that helped you to succeed. It is just as important to examine experiences you would not like to repeat.

Combining the desirable experiences into a formula will result in methods, skills, or techniques that continuously get results when applied to your personal, spiritual, family, social, business, professional, or civic life. You can develop methods, skills, and techniques that continuously get results when applied regarding any activity, service, or product with which you are concerned. Success is achieved and maintained by those who try and keep trying with a Positive Mental Attitude.

You, too, will find the health, happiness, wealth, and success you seek.

Be proud! Be proud of your achievements, your family, your religion, your country, and all that is good, but be modest and have a sense of humility. One can take justifiable pride in achievement that's positive, but boastfulness of that achievement can be negative.

In the English language, one word can have many different meanings, both positive and negative, and *Pride* is an excellent example. Pride is a proper sense of personal dignity, worth, honor, and self-respect. This is positive, when applied to something of which one can be justly proud. But in the negative sense, pride is listed first among the seven deadly sins. Proverbs 16:18 says: "Pride goes before destruction and a haughty spirit before a fall."

Negative pride is an undue sense of one's own superiority, inordinate self-esteem, conceit; in fact, the synonyms for pride in a negative sense are arrogance, haughtiness, insolence, overbearingness, superciliousness, disdain. The antonyms are humility and modesty.

SELF-TEST

∾

Consider the following situations:

1. You have submitted an ambitious plan to reorganize your department and are about to meet with the people who will make the final decision. What do you concentrate on before the meeting?

   a) Routine details so that your nervousness does not overwhelm you.

   b) All the tough questions you will be asked and the objections you expect upper management to have.

   c) The benefits that will arise from your recommendations and how easy it will be to explain them.

2. Your spouse has just been offered an important promotion. The new position will mean increased salary and opportunity for further advancement, but also a greater workload. What do you contribute to the discussion about accepting the job?

   a) "Do whatever you think is best, dear."

   b) "Just remember what happened to the last person who got that job. He couldn't take the pressure and got fired."

   c) "This is a terrific opportunity, and I'm sure you can

handle it. If you want to go for it, I'm behind you all the way."

3. As head of the local PTA, you are surprised when the popular school principal announces she is leaving to go back to college. The superintendent of schools asks you to serve on the committee to select a replacement. What attitude do you bring to the hiring process?

a) Decide that one principal is the same as another and defer to other committee members.

b) State clearly that you believe it will be impossible to find someone as good as the last principal and remind everyone that they should expect to hear complaints about whoever they choose.

c) Recognize that good principals can be found and that the previous one gives you an excellent standard to use, but that each candidate will have different strengths and the key will be finding the one who is best suited to your school's needs.

4. Your daily commute takes forty-five minutes each way. How do you spend the time?

a) Listening to music.

b) Listening to people complain about everything on talk radio.

c) Envisioning what you will accomplish today and how it will bring you closer to your major goals in life.

Napoleon Hill once said, "The only thing you can control for certain in any situation is your reaction to it."

If you make a habit of adopting an optimistic outlook in every situation, you will find that you are helping to create that outcome by everything you say and do.

Every one of us knows that little voice that pops up once in a while and says, "This won't work," or "Failure is just around the corner." You can tame that little voice by concentrating on positive thoughts, but it is persistent, so you cannot simply ignore it. You may think that by changing what you are thinking about you can make the voice go away, but that doesn't really work. You have to drown it out with the positive voice that says what you know can be true. And you do a great favor to others when you add your positive voice to their thoughts. This is why the "a" responses above do not reflect PMA.

Everyone's mental attitude is contagious. This is why you do no one—including yourself—any favors by harping on potential problems. The "b" responses above represent negative mental attitudes that are quickly communicated to the people around you, sabotaging their efforts and their reactions to your own efforts. It is inevitable that a negative thought will sometimes crop up in your head. But do not thoughtlessly give it voice. You should examine it to see if it identifies a real problem, but nine times out of ten, the only action it will require is replacing it with a positive alternative.

Don't make the mistake of thinking that adopting a happy outlook is putting on blinders. History is full of examples of people who ignored all the reasons why something was doomed to failure and did it anyway: Robert Fulton, Thomas Edison, the Wright brothers. To use an example from Dennis Kimbro, the co-author with Napoleon Hill of *Think and Grow Rich: A Black Choice*, people may tell you that the sun has gone down, but they are wrong. The sun never truly goes down. It may be night where you stand, but on much of the earth the sun shines bright.

Why Act Any Other Way?

Susan Jeffers, author of the book *Feel the Fear and Do It Anyway*, was having dinner with a friend, trying to make her dining companion see the positive side of something, when the other woman remarked, "You're beginning to sound like Pollyanna."

Jeffers remembers, "I blurted out, 'What's so terrible about Pollyanna, anyway? What's wrong with feeling good about life despite the obstacles in your way? What's wrong with looking at the sun instead of seeing doom and gloom? What's wrong with trying to see good in everything? *Nothing* is wrong with it!' I asserted. 'In fact,' I added incredulously, "why would anyone *resist* thinking that way?' "

Only you can choose the attitude you adopt in a situation. If you wallow in the mud of negative thinking, it will stick to you and everyone around you will know. Choose instead to fix your mind on the things you want and the certainty that you will get them. If you have to worry, worry positively.

Bonus: Teach yourself the infectious power of happiness by standing in front of the mirror and smiling at yourself. It's okay if you feel a little awkward at first, maybe even better if you're tempted to laugh, because then you will smile for real. But just seeing yourself smile is certain to give you an inkling of the happiness that something so simple can bring. Now imagine what can happen if you share that smile with someone else.

∽ Words from the Wise ∽

"A merry heart doeth good like a medicine."
—Proverbs 17:22

"Cheerfulness keeps up a kind of daylight in the mind, and fills it with a steady and perpetual serenity."—Joseph Addison

"Assume a virtue, if you have it not."
—William Shakespeare

"Give me a man who sings at his work."
—Thomas Carlyle

"If you want a quality, act as if you already had it. Try the 'as if' technique."—William James

"If we really want to live, we'd better start at once to try."—W. H. Auden

"Use your weaknesses; aspire to the strength."
—Laurence Olivier

"Be bold—and mighty forces will come to your aid."—Basil King

"Peak performers are people who approach any set of circumstances with the attitude that they can get it to turn out the way they want it to. Not once in a while. Regularly. They can count on themselves."
—Charles Garfield

7

Step Six: Form a Habit of Tolerance

Keep an open mind toward people. Try to like and accept people just as they are instead of demanding or wishing that they be as you want them to be. Look for the good in others and learn to like people. Many years ago, Napoleon Hill wrote the following essay on intolerance:

> When the dawn of Intelligence shall spread over the eastern horizon of human progress, and Ignorance and Superstition shall have left their last footprints on the sands of time, it will be recorded in the last chapter of the book of man's crimes that his most grievous sin was that of intolerance.
>
> The bitterest intolerance grows out of religious, racial, and economic prejudices and differences of opinion. How long, O God, until we poor mortals

will understand the folly of trying to destroy one another because we are of different religious beliefs and racial tendencies?

Our allotted time on this earth is but a fleeting moment. Like a candle, we are lighted, shine for a moment, and flicker out. Why can we not learn to so live during this brief earthly visit that when the great Caravan called Death draws up and announces this visit completed, we will be ready to fold our tents and silently follow out into the great unknown without fear and trembling?

I am hoping that I will find no Jews or Gentiles, Catholics or Protestants, Germans, Englishmen, or Frenchmen when I shall have crossed the bar to the other side. I am hoping that I will find there only human Souls, Brothers and Sisters all, unmarked by race, creed, or color, for I shall want to be done with intolerance so I may rest in peace throughout eternity.

Love and affection generate the mental and physical environment in which PMA can flourish. Every day, do a good deed. It's good advice for Boy Scouts, and it's good advice for us.

This is a true story: There was a New England high school student who was an excellent gymnast. He was en route to a championship meet. As he drove over a certain bridge, he noticed a gap in the railing. He stopped and saw a truck in the river below. The accident had just happened, the truck was still sinking, and the driver was struggling to get out.

Intolerance's Ugly Head

One of the saddest effects of intolerance is that people who have experienced it often spread it around to some other group. The examples of countries like the former Yugoslavia show us how easily intolerant attitudes can tear a society apart.

One of the best ways to see how foolish intolerance is comes in examining old social attitudes that once held sway. For instance, for many years, it was believed that no one could be elected President of the United States who was Catholic or had been divorced. But two of our most popular presidents in recent memory defy these beliefs: John F. Kennedy was Catholic, and Ronald Reagan had been divorced.

Be sure that you don't let intolerant ideas you have absorbed from other people limit your own ideas of what you can achieve. There must always be a first person to cross a barrier. Why can't it be you?

The high school youth took off only his shoes, then dived into the swirling waters below. The panicked truck driver couldn't open the door. The high schooler motioned to the driver to roll the window down, for the truck was almost completely submerged. The driver did roll the window down and the youth, from his years of training and exercise, used every muscle and ounce of strength to pull the driver from the truck. He pulled the driver to the surface and swam to the shore, thereby saving the trucker's life.

The gymnast never did show up for the state meet

that night, but it didn't matter, for school officials had barred him from the competition anyhow because he had long hair.

The moral: don't judge a man's character by the length of his hair.

Acts of human kindness condition you and others for the growth of PMA. To be happy, make others happy!

LEARN BY DOING
Form a Habit of Tolerance

The secret of accepting people for what they are is to act as if you do already. Think of one person you have trouble accepting, and write that person's name below:

Name: _____

Now ask yourself, if I did accept that person just as he or she is, how would I behave? What would I actually do? Visualize your answer in concrete terms. Then do it. Most people let their feelings master them. They assume they cannot behave lovingly toward someone, or tolerantly, or whatever, until they have first conjured up the correct feeling of love, or tolerance, or whatever. This is backward. Your new understanding of a Positive Mental Attitude now equips you to realize that you can master your feelings! You can choose to act as though you were feeling whatever you want to feel. The intriguing aspect to this is that the feelings come trotting along obediently afterward.

SELF-TEST

Consider the following questions:

1. *The office next to yours is occupied by a rowdy sales manager. Every time one of her reps makes a sales goal, she whoops for joy and raises a ruckus. The whole office stops working and stares at her. What is your response?*

a) Keep your office door shut.
b) Tell her she is disrupting office discipline and ask her to find another way to celebrate. Maybe she could send the rep some e-mail.
c) Do something that acknowledges her enthusiasm, so that you share in every good thing that happens to her.

2. *Your son announces he is engaged to a young woman, whom you meet and like, but then you discover that her parents are actively involved in a political party with aims you heartily oppose. What is your response?*

a) Do your best to avoid them.
b) Tell them that they had better not bring up any of their ridiculous ideas around you.
c) Make friends with them on the basis of your common bond and realize that you have an opportunity to get to know people you might otherwise never share anything with.

3. A petition circulates in your neighborhood to force lo-cal officials to do something about a house down the street where the yard is never mowed and garbage accu-mulates. What do you do?

  a) Stay out of other people's problems and don't sign the petition.
  b) Sign the petition.
  c) Offer to pay a visit to your neighbor and explain what is troubling people and ask whether there is any-thing you can do to help remedy the situation before involving the government.

4. A new woman joins your department. She does her work well, but other employees seem to avoid her once a rumor circulates that she is a lesbian. How do you respond?

  a) Ignore the rumor.
  b) Tell her what other people are saying and suggest she might be happier working for another company.
  c) Invite her to lunch and get to know her better. Tell her how pleased you are with her work and ask her to let you know if she has any problems getting along in the office.

Tolerance can be a difficult issue, especially given the polarized times we live in. No matter the topic, many people have strong feelings that sometimes overwhelm their better judgment and don't allow them to see the is-sues at hand. Having PMA does not mean that you have to embrace the principles of everyone you meet, but it does mean that you must take a long, hard look at your reactions to those people. Ask yourself, do my feelings have anything to do with the way I interact with this person? Does issue X relate to selling widgets, being a good neighbor, or living by the Golden Rule?

Tolerance is not a passive part of PMA, or of any part of life. As the earlier example of Reverend Martin Niemoller in Nazi Germany showed, the forces of intolerance depend on the inaction of good people. The "a" responses above largely represent that kind of response. In the first example, though, avoiding a situation that makes you uncomfortable actually robs you of an opportunity to learn from someone else and to share in the benefits of contagious enthusiasm.

You will never approach anything like that kind of understanding if you attempt to drive additional wedges between yourself and people with whom you do not agree. The best you may be able to achieve with them is an amiable truce, but even that will be impossible if you lay down the kind of challenge the "b" responses represent. Your every interaction with them will be poisoned by the threat of confrontation, and that is a sure way to distract yourself from the positive thoughts you need to cultivate in reaching your goals.

Tolerance will not eliminate the possibility that conflict will occur, but if your actions are typical of the "c" responses above, you will have shown other people that you respect them. You can rely on their respect being returned. That simple exchange opens up a world of ways in which you are able to work with people whom you might never otherwise even speak to. The differences of opinion between you will likely remain, but who knows, you may gain enough respect from the other person to win a convert to your way of thinking. With PMA, all things are possible.

Bonus: The little trick you learned here is also the key to the biblical comment to "love your enemy." How do I love my enemy? By acting as if I did already. Lo and behold, the feeling will come afterward. Do you have any enemies you want to try this on? Write the name below, and try it.

Name: _____

At the end of your day, consider this prayer:

Have you made someone happy or made someone sad?
What have you done with the day that you had?
God gave it to you to do just as you would.
Did you do what was wicked or do what was good?
Did you hand out a smile or just give them a frown?
Did you lift someone up or push someone down?
Did you lighten some load or some progress impede?
Did you look for a rose or just gather weed?
What did you do with your beautiful day?
God gave it to you.
Did you throw it away?

(Author Unknown)

∽ Words from the Wise ∽

"It takes a wise man to recognize a wise man."
—Xenophanes

"Grant that we may not so much seek to be understood as to understand."—St. Francis of Assisi

> *"Do all the good you can*
> *By all the means you can*
> *In all the ways you can*
> *In all the places you can*
> *At all the times you can*
> *To all the people you can*
> *As long as you ever can."*
> —John Wesley

"Nothing is ever lost by courtesy. It is the cheapest of pleasures, costs nothing, and conveys much. It pleases him who gives and receives and thus, like mercy, is twice blessed."—Erastus Wiman

"A great many people think they are thinking when they are merely rearranging their prejudices."
—William James

8

Step Seven: Give Yourself Positive Suggestions

Condition your mind so that it will express a Positive Mental Attitude at all times. You must realize that you translate into physical reality the thoughts and attitudes that you dwell on. You have probably heard the saying, "Tell me what you think about, and I'll tell you who you are." This is an echo of William James's statement, "We become what we think about most of the time."

Your subconscious mind can and will communicate to your conscious mind. Concepts, ideas, solutions to problems—all these are offerings waiting to come up to your conscious knowledge. And more, for your mind is a storehouse of powers known and unknown. Your conscious and subconscious mind can work together in harmony only if you learn how to affect your mind intelligently. In their book *Success Through a Positive*

Mental Attitude, Napoleon Hill and W. Clement Stone explain that in order for you to deliberately maintain a Positive Mental Attitude, you must control the external stimuli your mind receives. There are three forms of control you can exert: suggestion, self-suggestion, and auto-suggestion.

Suggestion

Any stimulus sent through your brain through your five senses—sight, hearing, touch, taste, or smell—is a form of suggestion. All of these are pathways by which external elements influence you every day of your life. Everything you come in contact with is recorded in your subconscious mind by your five senses. As much as it is within your control, see to it that what enters your five senses is wholesome and gratifying. Take time for beauty.

Self-Suggestion

Self-suggestion is the process of purposely and deliberately offering stimuli to yourself in the form of seeing, hearing, feeling, tasting, or smelling. Use mental pictures or thoughts as a form of self-suggestion. Under "suggestion," you were warned to see to it that what enters your five senses is wholesome and gratifying. Perhaps the thought occurs to you: "But the world has an unavoidable ugliness in it." This is just where self-suggestion can come into play, and the underlying philosophy of PMA: look for the good in whatever you see or hear or taste or smell or feel. The more you purposely repeat a message to yourself, and the more emotion and belief you imbue it with, the more effectively it is implanted in your subconscious mind. By building up successful thought patterns, you can put the same great truth to work for you as so many successful people have done.

Do successful people know some special secret for living? They look for the funny side of things. From this day on, you will too. From this day on, you will laugh off your shortcomings. From this day on, you will refuse to take yourself too seriously. From this day on, you will constantly cultivate your sense of humor by finding something to laugh at each day when you feel a need to relax from tension. From this day on, you will try to attract new friends by a more cheerful attitude. From this day on, you will use humor as an aid to the solution of your problems.

Auto-Suggestion

Auto-suggestion is the transmission and communication of information stored in the subconscious mind back to your conscious mind. This information returns to you in the form of ideas, dreams, feelings, concepts, principles, solutions, and thoughts. When you deliberately feed your mind with good, wholesome thoughts and information, and keep yourself in the proper frame of mind, you are supplying the subconscious with nourishing material to feed back to you. You condition your mind's output by the input you give it.

Computer programmers have an acronym, GIGO, that stands for "Garbage In, Garbage Out." If a computer gets bad data fed into it, it will produce bad information. Your mind works the same way. Make your mental programming on the basis of NINO: Nourishment In, Nourishment Out. And the output is the automatic maintenance of a Positive Mental Attitude.

Visualize Your Gains

Bob Paris is an international bodybuilding champion, a former Mr. Olympia, and a man who acknowledges in the introduction to one of his training books Napoleon Hill's famous maxim, "Whatever the mind can conceive and believe, it can achieve."

Paris incorporates the power of self-suggestion and autosuggestion into his workout routines and insists that they are important for everyone who wants to achieve maximum benefit from the work they put into training. "You should learn to perfect the exercises and feel the muscle being worked," he says. He calls this "finding" the muscle, so that at its peak contraction, he is focused on the work it is doing, literally visualizing it growing and becoming stronger.

Paris advises, "Any time you aren't 'finding' your muscle during a workout, stop . . . to get back in touch with the right feeling." Good advice for everything you do with PMA.

LEARN BY DOING
Give Yourself Positive Suggestions

Suggestion, self-suggestion, and auto-suggestion are matters of habit learned by attention. Suggestion and self-suggestion are the new habits you can build; they are food for the mind. Auto-suggestion is the one that requires attention: learning to rejoice when your positive mental attitude results in some new thought or feeling. Practice each of them daily.

Suggestion: Make it a rule to treat one of your five senses to something positive and valuable each day. Study a flower. Visit a bakery and inhale the aroma. Go to a concert, or listen to something beautiful on the radio. Taste the full flavor of bread as though it were the only food you would have that day. Feel the texture of bark on a tree. What are you going to do today to feed your senses with positive nourishment?

*Suggestion:*_____

_____

Auto-suggestion: Conscious awareness is the skill you need when it comes to auto-suggestion. Many people take the ideas and concepts and solutions and good feelings they have for granted, but you won't. You will rejoice—hey, that's just the kind of person you are. Keep a record for a while of the development of a Positive Mental Attitude in you: What "good food" has your subconscious fed you today?

*Auto-suggestion:*_____

_____

SELF-TEST

❧

Consider the following situations.

1. You've just learned that the promotion you very much wanted has gone to someone else. How do you react?

a) Get back to working as quickly as possible. Don't dwell on defeat.

b) Consider resigning or at least looking for a job where your efforts will be appreciated.

c) Congratulate the other person, then spend some time reminding yourself of all the things that have gone as you wanted them by reviewing your file of achievements.

2. The fight you had this morning with your spouse got out of hand, and you both said some harsh things. You are the first one home at the end of the day. How do you react when your other half arrives?

a) Pretend nothing is wrong.

b) Insist on hashing things out before another moment passes.

c) Suggest a quiet dinner someplace you both enjoy to remind yourselves that you are partners who share many good things.

3. You have agreed to chaperone an outing of your church youth group, but at the last minute you find out that it involves Rollerblading. You've never been on skates in your life. What is your attitude?

a) Show up ready to fall down.
b) Back out of the commitment.
c) Rent a pair of skates a few days ahead of the trip and do some practicing in your driveway.

4. It's your first day in your new office. What do you put on the wall where you can see it most easily?

a) Your diploma.
b) Your job description.
c) Your list of self-motivators and reinforcing thoughts.

You must always act to be certain that you are giving yourself the right kind of stimulation to maintain PMA. In any given situation, such as with the "a" responses, it may seem like bravery not to admit that you need a little reinforcement or encouragement, but this only leaves you out on a limb when upsets occur. PMA is not a *passive* mental attitude—it is an active one.

You must also guard against giving yourself any suggestion that you are likely to fail or encounter disappointment. The "b" responses are all ways of telling yourself that failure is close at hand, and the more you go looking for failure, the easier it is for failure to find you.

The "c" responses represent taking control of a situation so that you stimulate your mind to think of success, of your ability to achieve things, to ride out and conquer complications. Naysayers might call them whistling in the wind, but with just a little experience with PMA, you will know that you are capable of whatever task you set for yourself.

Bonus: Keep a record of each time you notice Auto-suggestion working for you. It may provide a solution to a problem, or an idea for a new activity. As your record grows longer, you'll have evidence of how your mental attitude is affecting your progress toward success.

❧ Words from the Wise ❧

"If you treat a person as he is, he will stay as he is; but if you treat him as if he were what he ought to be, he will become what he ought to be and could be."—Johann Goethe

"Human felicity is produced not so much by great pieces of good fortune that seldom happen, as by little advantages that occur every day."
—Benjamin Franklin

"Put vim, force, vitality into every movement of your body. Let your very atmosphere be that of [one] who is . . . determined to stand for something, and to be somebody. . . . Dare to step out of the crowd and blaze your own path."
—Orison Swett Marden

"What your mind can conceive and believe, you can achieve with PMA."—Napoleon Hill

"Aspire to greatness. Each of us is going to travel the road of life's adventure only once, but once is enough if you do it right."—J. Warren McClure

"What would you attempt to do if you knew you could not fail?"—Robert Schuller

"My philosophy is that only you are responsible for your life, but doing the best at this moment puts you in the best place for the next moment."
—Oprah Winfrey

9

Step Eight: Use Your Power of Prayer

You may be uncertain about the existence of God, or even convinced that he does not exist. But it will only take a little optimistic experimenting to make you a believer in the power of prayer.

It doesn't matter what name you give to the Higher Power to which you pray, even if it is simply the Universe, as long as you admit that the entire world is set up according to an orderly process. You see this process in the fact that the sun rises, that oaks grow from acorns not from apple seeds, and that the planets, sun, and the stars move through the vast emptiness of space in a regular and predictable pattern.

Once you acknowledge the order of the world, you will see that it can be understood, and thus changed by acting within its rules. Prayer is the process by which you acknowledge your place within that order, and begin to prepare yourself to change it. If you acknowledge God and his benevolence, so much the better. But even if you doubt it—and that doubt will not last long—you will still prepare yourself for achievement through prayer, such as the following:

> O Father, hear my morning prayer
> Thine aid impart to me
> That I may make my life today
> Acceptable to Thee
> I do not ask to choose my path
> Lord, bless me in Thy way
> Inspire each thought and
> Make me a blessing today
> Help us to do the things we should
> To be to others kind and good
> In all we do, in work or play
> To grow more loving every day
> Finally, brothers, whatsoever things are true
> Whatsoever things are just
> Whatsoever things are pure
> Whatsoever things are lovely
> Whatsoever things are of good report
> If there be any virtue and if there be any praise
> Think on these things.

When you pray, have faith and believe in that which you ask for. In every storm, what an asylum has a soul in prayer.

Archbishop User preached, "We have assurance that

we shall be heard in what we pray because we pray to that God that heareth prayer and is the reward of all that come unto him."

Believe that the Almighty wants to hear all that is on your mind, no matter how small or big a matter it may seem. Our prayer and God's mercy are like two buckets in a well; while the one ascends, the other descends. Prayer is a shield to the soul, a sacrifice to God, and a scourge for Satan.

The Creative Power of Prayer

Mel Ziegler was one of the founders of the Banana Republic chain of clothing stores, and then of the highly successful company called The Republic of Tea, which changed the way Americans think about and drink this ancient beverage.

Ziegler has twice found and ridden waves of changes in consumer tastes. Some might say he creates trends. But listen to what he has to say about inspiration and consider how closely it comes to prayer.

"Creation is a *projection* of something that already exists . . . ," he writes. "The great mystery we know as the 'creative process' is, in fact, the stirring of the unborn in its search for a friendly place to be born."

By opening yourself to the power of prayer, what ideas will find themselves being born in your mind?

We must also remember that "no" can be an answer to a prayer. Pray to thy Father which is in secret, and thy Father which seeth in secret shall reward thee openly.

Time spent on the knees in prayer will do more to remedy heart strain and nerve worry than anything else. The simple heart that freely asks in love obtains.

Like an echo from a ruined castle, prayer is an echo from the ruined human soul of the sweetest promise of God. Reaching deep within yourself, as you do when you pray, is what opens the storehouse of infinity to you. You can and you will receive direction from God. Call it insight if you must, but the truth is the same.

When someone once asked Henry Drummond how one can know the will of God, Drummond opened his Bible and read these directions from the flyleaf:

FIRST, pray.

SECOND, think.

THIRD, talk to wise people but don't regard their judgment as final.

FOURTH, beware of putting forth of your own will, but don't be too afraid of it. God never unnecessarily thwarts a man's nature and liking. It is a mistake to think that His will is always in the line of the disagreeable.

FIFTH, meanwhile, do the next thing, for doing God's will in small things is the best preparation for doing it in great things.

SIXTH, when decision and action are necessary, go ahead.

SEVENTH, you will probably not find out until afterward, perhaps long afterward, that you have been led at all.

The prayers that work the greatest good in you are the ones you utter, really believing that they will be answered.

LEARN BY DOING
Use Your Power of Prayer

Episcopal priest Sam Shoemaker introduced a plan—now called the "Pittsburgh Experiment"—in the 1950s. He and a group of businessmen met regularly. Some of them believed in God, some were agnostic, some flat out did not believe. Shoemaker asked each of them to join with him in an experiment, to approach the whole question of whether God existed and was concerned for individuals' welfare, with an open mind for thirty days. During that time, he suggested, each man should start his day with this prayer:

"Good morning, God. What have you got for me today? I want to be a part of it."

Then Shoemaker asked that each man just keep tuned in to what happened, with an open mind to the possibility that evidence of God in their lives would really come through. Every one of these men, at the end of the thirty-day "experiment," had positive results to report. Every one of them felt certain that they had seen evidence of God involved in their lives.

Try the "Pittsburgh Experiment" prayer yourself, believing that it will be answered. It will be. You might keep a thirty-day journal of God's activity in your life.

SELF-TEST

Consider the following situations:

1. What is the focus of your morning routine before going to work?

   a) Dressing and eating with brisk efficiency.
   b) Mentally reviewing the potential problems you will face that day.
   c) Spending time in reflective prayer, giving thanks for the opportunities you have been presented, and seeking wisdom to best take advantage of them.

2. You and your spouse have been considering the purchase of a new house. The step will stretch your resources, but you believe that it could be a wise move financially. Both of you have spent much time in contemplative prayer. Then comes a series of events that seems to suggest the purchase would be an even greater strain than you realized: interest rates rise, homes around you are selling at depressed prices, and your spouse's company announces a downsizing. What do you decide?

   a) Flip a coin.
   b) Charge ahead with the purchase before anything else goes wrong.

c) Decide that the wisest course is to wait until you are in a better position to afford a new home.

3. *You have prayed fervently for a new school in your neighborhood, though the local district has little money for new construction. In your heart you are convinced that the new school is important and necessary. What steps do you take?*

a) Trust that your prayers will be answered.

b) Threaten a recall campaign against board members if they do not vote for a new school.

c) Organize a group of parents and concerned citizens to lobby for the school and to present evidence of its importance to the board.

4. *Suddenly you find yourself promoted to head a disorganized department at your company. There is much work to be done and resistance will likely be strong. How do you shape your prayers?*

a) Use the same formula you always have.

b) Pray for victory over those who oppose you.

c) Express gratitude for the opportunity and responsibility you have been given, and ask for wisdom to make the very most of them.

Prayer's power is twofold. On one hand, you open yourself to the wisdom of Higher Authority, the Infinite Intelligence that orders the universe. The contemplative aspect of prayer allows you to see solutions and find wisdom that once seemed beyond your grasp. In this respect, prayer's power is *external*, for it draws to you things you do not presently possess.

Prayer's *internal* power is the effect it has on your mind. By adopting a grateful, optimistic attitude in your prayers, you reinforce the power of self-suggestion you learned about in Step #7. If you begin your day with prayers, and return to them several times throughout the day, you connect this self-suggestion to the most powerful force in the universe: the great Intelligence that created it.

The first two "a" responses above fail to acknowledge the basic existence of this power. You must devote time to prayer each day. If at first it seems a chore to set aside a few moments, you'll soon find you welcome the calmness and centering that prayer provides, even in the midst of a hectic morning. And once you do embrace prayer, you'll recognize the foolishness of random decision making when you have the wisdom of creation to call upon.

The dynamic power of prayer also requires that it cannot be exercised by rote. The second two "a" responses touch on the mistake of simply assuming that what you pray for will happen simply because you pray for it. You must clearly and thoughtfully adapt your prayers to your changing circumstances, and you must be willing to act in pursuit of the things you pray for. PMA requires that you be willing to work and to take risks to achieve anything. Your prayers should never be a wish list; rather make them a work list of challenges you are prepared to tackle.

It is wise and important to pray for help in overcoming obstacles, but foolish to make your prayers a time when you concentrate on what you do not want to happen. The "b" responses above all represent a misuse of prayer and what you hope to gain by it. Never attempt to call down revenge on your enemies or to remind Infinite Intelligence (and yourself) of what can go wrong in your day.

The "c" responses represent the proper approach to prayer and the answers it brings. If you always adopt an attitude of thanksgiving for the blessings you have already received, it will be easier for you to recognize when prayer tells you that the time is not right for a particular choice. Any disappointment you feel will fall into the proper perspective when you frame your prayers as a reminder of the benefits you already enjoy.

Bonus: Henry Drummond's seven suggestions for knowing the will of God can work for you, too.

FIRST, what is the issue about which you are going to pray?

_____

_____

SECOND, after you have prayed, what thoughts have come to you about it?

_____

_____

THIRD, what did the wise people you talked to say about the matter?

_____

_____

FOURTH, what are your own inclinations in this matter?

_____

_____

FIFTH, meanwhile, what is "the next thing" for you to do?

_____

_____

SIXTH, do any decisions or actions suggest themselves?

_____

_____

SEVENTH, see what happens (and make a celebration record of it here).

_____

_____

∽ Words from the Wise ∽

"He that loveth little, prayeth little. He that loveth much, prayeth much."—St. Augustine

"Prayer is a sincere, sensible, affectionate pouring out of the soul to God."—John Bunyan

"I've been driven many times to my knees by the overwhelming conviction that I had nowhere else to go. My own wisdom and all of that about me seemed insufficient for that day."
—Abraham Lincoln

"Let prayer be the key of the morning and the bolt of the evening."—Matthew Henry

"Prayer is the gate of heaven."—Thomas Brooks

"It is so natural for a man to pray that no theory can prevent him from doing so."
—James Freeman Clark

"Prayer is the first breath of divine life, it is the pulse of the believing soul."—T. Scott

"Whatsoever we beg of God, let us also work for it."—Jeremy Scott

"As in poetry, so in prayer, the whole subject matter should be furnished by the heart."
—Edward Payson

"Your greatest power lies in the power of prayer."
—W. Clement Stone

10

Step Nine: Set Goals

It is up to you to decide what you want from life. When you decide, then you can take possession of your mind and use it to reach goals of your own choosing. And you can literally accomplish anything—as long as it does not violate the laws of God or the rights of others. You can experience the thrill of knowing that you can achieve any goal or objective you set out to accomplish.

Setting goals is one way to keep your mind on the things you want, and off the things you don't want, which is what Step #2 urged. You need to learn to set short- and long-term goals on a daily basis. This is very important. Write your goals on a sheet of paper. Visualize yourself achieving those goals. Constantly refer to them in an expectant, positive manner.

The starting point for achieving goals is found in the six-letter word *desire*.

Determine

Evaluate

Set

Identify

Repeat

Each day

Make the Choice

In their book, *Think and Grow Rich: A Black Choice,* Dennis Kimbro and Napoleon Hill point out how important having a goal is to making something out of your life. Among the examples they cite:

- Gwendolyn Brooks cannot recall a time when she did not want to be a poet. At fifteen she was publishing poems and winning praise that continued as she became the first Black person to win a Pulitzer Prize.
- Florence Griffith-Joyner came in second place at the 1984 Olympics. She decided it wasn't good enough and set herself the goal of winning three gold medals at the next games. She did it, and set world records each time.

You may tell yourself you are going to be somebody, but until you define exactly what that means, you are only going to be the same somebody you already are.

D-E-S-I-R-E is the method you can use to set and achieve any goal you choose. Determine and fix in your mind EXACTLY what you desire. Be specific. Evaluate and determine EXACTLY what you will give in return. Set a definite date as to when you intend to possess it. Identify your desire with a definite plan for carrying it out and achieving your objective. Put your plan into action at once. I recommend that you memorize the three words *Do It Now* and repeat those three words fifty times in the morning, fifty times at night, some time during the day, with enthusiasm and with rapidity, for a week or ten days until they're ingrained in the subconscious mind. Then, in time of need you will immediately get into action.

Success is achieved by those who try. Where there is nothing to lose by trying and a great deal to gain if successful, by all means, try . . . DO IT NOW!

Repeat your step-by-step plan in writing. Write out clearly and concisely EXACTLY what you want, EXACTLY when you want to achieve it, and EXACTLY what you intend to give in return. Be precise—vagueness is the death knell of goal achievement.

Each and every day, morning and evening, read your written statement aloud. AS YOU READ, VISUALIZE YOURSELF IN POSSESSION OF YOUR OBJECTIVE. SEE IT. FEEL IT. BELIEVE IT.

LEARN BY DOING
Set Goals

Set a goal right now. In doing so, follow the D-E-S-I-R-E
formula you have just learned.
Determine: What do you want? Be definite.

_____

_____

Evaluate: What will you give in return?

_____

_____

Set a date: When will you have what you want?

_____

_____

Identify: Make a plan. What will you do at once?

_____

_____

Repeat your step-by-step plan in writing. (You may need
more space than is allowed here.)

Step 1. _____

Step 2. _____

Step 3. _____

Step 4. _____

Step 5. _____

Each and every day, morning and evening, read your written statement aloud. Visualize yourself already in possession of your objective as you read.

SELF-TEST

Answer the following questions:

1. Which best describes your goals?

a) Can't really describe them.
b) Not getting fired, avoiding bankruptcy, not getting sick, minimizing conflict at home.
c) A clear plan for career advancement, definite financial targets, regular activity to increase your health, greater and deeper partnership with your spouse.

2. What are you doing to achieve your goals?

a) Fantasizing about what life would be like.
b) Struggling to avoid losing ground and dealing with any crisis as soon as it arises.
c) Following a written plan, which I review daily, that outlines immediate, mid-range, and long-term steps.

3. What do you expect to give in return for achieving your goals?

a) No idea.
b) As little as possible, since it's been hard enough to get this far. I need to get rich quick.
c) As much time, energy, devotion, service to my community, and whatever other specifics are required.

4. *When did you last review your goals?*

  a) Can't review them because they aren't set.
  b) In the midst of the last crisis.
  c) Today, as I do every day.

Nowhere is the weakness of a passive approach to life more evident than in the wheel-spinning that comes as a result of not setting goals. You can't get someplace you've never been before without planning your trip. Any "a" answers above should immediately explain to you why you are dissatisfied with your current situation in life. How can you complain that things aren't to your liking if you don't know what it is you really want?

The trap that many people fall into is telling themselves that they do have goals—and then expressing all those goals in negative terms. As you have already learned, concentrating on what you don't want to happen almost ensures that it will happen. The first two "b" answers illustrate this kind of negative mental attitude.

As with prayer, you must also acknowledge that even positively expressed goals are not achieved by wishing. You must take an active role in their execution, and be willing to return something for whatever you hope to gain. Whether like Henry Ford you become immensely wealthy by providing automobiles to a nation, or like Henry Fonda you achieve great fame by offering extraordinary entertainment, you must give in order to get. This is the lesson of the third "b" response.

The fourth "b" response underscores the importance of staying focused on your goals. Every day you will make many decisions that can affect their possible realization. To do this best, you must regularly remind yourself of what your goals are so that you can act in pursuit of them.

The "c" responses represent the focused approach to living that PMA goal-setting provides. You know and concentrate your thoughts on what you want. You have a plan for achieving your ambitions, and you review it often. In this way, all your actions and prayers move you forward toward a chosen target.

It is likely that at several points in your life you will consider changing your goals. Do not be distressed when this happens. We all gain wisdom and find opportunities we never dreamed existed. If you are aware of what you want, and you know from experience that you can pursue it, you will be able to analyze these chances, and if you so choose, embrace them with confidence. That is the essence of PMA.

Bonus: Keep a slip of paper in your pocket with your goals for the day written on it. It will be a reminder every time you reach for change or your keys. No pockets? Then keep it where you will encounter it frequently during the day.

❧ Words from the Wise ❧

"A journey of a thousand miles begins with a single step."—Lao-Tzu

"And whatsoever ye do, do it heartily."
—Colossians 3:23

"Every noble work is at first impossible."
—Thomas Carlyle

"The great thing in this world is not so much where we are, but in what direction we are moving."
—Oliver Wendell Holmes

"Four steps to achievement: plan purposefully, prepare prayerfully, proceed positively, pursue persistently."—William A. Ward

"Most people don't plan to fail; they fail to plan."
—John L. Beckley

"There are risks and costs to a program of action, but they are far less than the long-range risks and costs of comfortable inaction."—John F. Kennedy

"Strong lives are motivated by dynamic purposes."
—Kenneth Hildebrand

"You've got to be very careful if you don't know where you are going, because you might not get there."—Yogi Berra

"I always wanted to be somebody, but I should have been more specific."—Lily Tomlin

11

Step Ten: Study, Think, and Plan Daily

You owe it to yourself to develop and maintain a Positive Mental Attitude in order to get from life everything that you desire.

A gentleman came up and pointed out to me that he had a lot of problems. He was very unhappy, even though he was successful in the sale of life insurance for a large eastern company. I asked him if he had inspirational self-help books, and his answer was that he had that kind of book in his library. Then I asked the question, "Do you read them?"

"No. I don't have the time," he said.

Now, the interesting thing is this: the successful person will make the time to do the important, specifically, to read and study a self-help book for the purpose of developing either financial wealth, success in his particular business or vocation, or the acquisition of good physical, mental, or moral health.

To accomplish this, it is important that EACH DAY you spend private time with yourself. This means at least fifteen to twenty minutes that you:

1. Think about your goals . . . with PMA.
2. Inspect your attitudes . . . with PMA.
3. Inspect your actions and your thinking . . . with PMA.
4. Read inspirational, self-help action material, even if it is only a paragraph, a page, or a chapter . . . with PMA.
5. Take time to study, to think, and to plan . . . with PMA.

LEARN BY DOING
Study, Think, and Plan Daily

Get yourself ready for a future lifetime of PMA excitement. What are you going to study? First, read an inspirational, self-help action editorial, article, book, or listen to an inspirational tape. All you need to do is take fifteen minutes, or if you want, just a short chapter, but try to understand what the author is trying to say. Use a dictionary if necessary. Determine what principles can be applied to you. Memorize self-motivators that you believe will help you. Select an environment where you can concentrate without being disturbed. Have a notepad and pencil or pen handy. Also, prepare yourself for the future by having a permanent notebook in which you write down resolutions, self-motivators, and ideas that should be reviewed with regularity. (If no other ideas come to you, this book will provide a rich resource for your repeated reading pleasure. There are also some suggestions in the Further Reading section at the back.)

My first study resource will be:

_____

W. Clement Stone once told me the difference between a novel and a self-help book is this: In a novel, the author writes the conclusion; in a self-help book, the reader writes the conclusion by the action he takes.

Get ready to write your own Success story. Find the time, make the time. Find the best time of day for you to set aside for your studying, thinking, and planning.

My studying/thinking/planning time will be:

_____

SELF-TEST

Ask yourself the following:

1. What commitment have I made to setting aside daily time for study, thinking, and planning my progress toward what I want?

  a) None.
  b) I take time whenever I can find it.
  c) I have a regular, daily period in which I am as free as possible from distractions.

2. Your friends invite you to get together at the end of a hectic day. You had planned to devote your free time to studying, planning, and thinking. What do you do?

  a) Go along.
  b) Tell yourself that what you really need is some relaxation, not more concentration.
  c) Agree to meet them after you've spent the time you need to in study, since you recognize that after a trying day, what you most need to do is reaffirm your commitment to your goals and strengthen your determination.

3. How do you select your reading materials?

  a) What reading materials?
  b) You look for anything that gives you an escape from the pressures of your day-to-day routine.

c) You select a variety of things, including biographies, inspirational works, self-improvement books or tapes, current events analysis, and great literature.

4. When you finish reading something, what do you do next?

a) Take a rest.
b) Move on to the next thing as soon as possible.
c) Take time to consider the implications of what you have encountered and where it might have ramifications in your own life. Make notes in your journal of insights you have gained, or particularly important quotations from the work.

If you approach the prospect of setting aside time for study and planning with PMA, you will almost immediately see how this time pays you tremendous benefits. It may seem like work at first, but remember what Thomas Edison said: "Most people do not recognize opportunity because it comes dressed in coveralls looking like work."

The "a" responses above represent a complete avoidance of the excitement and satisfaction that comes from carefully managed time. Why would anyone want to avoid thinking about the good things that will happen to them? If someone told you that you could double your knowledge in twenty minutes a day, wouldn't you grab those twenty minutes? Of course you would.

But you must make your commitment to the time you need. It's a fundamental part of what Dennis Conner called "the commitment to the commitment." The "b" responses demonstrate that there are plenty of distractions and excuses you will find to avoid the dedicated time you need for expanding your mind. If you fail to make and keep your commitment, you will find that the benefits you should be reaping will elude you, giving you another excuse to slack off in your promises to yourself.

The key to making study and planning time pay off is in challenging yourself. Explore new worlds, new philosophies, that cast new light on your situation. There are countless ways to do this. Is there some field of learning that has always fascinated you, but that you never explored? Why not begin now? It doesn't always have to appear to have an immediate benefit, but it probably will pay off in a way you can't anticipate. Suppose you decided you were interested in fine wine. As you read, you'd find yourself learning all kinds of things about geography, agriculture, history, food, different cultures, chemistry, even marketing. Which of those would you choose to explore next? What opportunity would you find there?

Remember that you're past the point of going to school because someone would punish you otherwise. The time you spend is time you choose to spend. Make it work for you.

Bonus: If you can find just twenty extra minutes in the morning and twenty extra minutes in the evening, that's nearly five hours a week you give to yourself. In a year you will have "found time" of nearly a week and a half extra. This is the time you can use for studying, thinking, planning, and prayer.

I urge you to take time out in your leisure hours to think with PMA, a positive mental attitude. With regard to creative thinking, I'm reminded of a true story that will interest you as it did me when it was told to me by W. Clement Stone. When Anthony Athanas opened Anthony's Pier 4 Restaurant in Boston some eight years ago, who do you suppose he invited as his guests on opening night? The President, governor, or television, movie, and theatrical personalities? No. He hosted every cabdriver and his wife or girlfriend in Boston that could attend. Anthony's Pier 4 is one of the most successful and profitable restaurants in America. When you are in Boston, step into a cab, as I have done, and ask the driver, "What's the best restaurant in town?" You can guess the answer. Anthony is successful because he found what he was looking for through taking the time to engage in study, thinking, and planning time.

Use these planning strategies:

1. Condition your mind. If you have had religious training, you will find it helpful to pray for guidance, for your greatest power lies in the power of prayer.

2. It's a good practice to think in terms of yourself, members of your family, your business or vocation, the acquisition of wealth, and whatever else is of interest to you. It's desirable to have specific objectives and time limits to achieve them. You can have

more than one definite purpose as long as your objectives are not in conflict with each other.

3. Ask yourself some questions. Write them down. For example, Anthony Athanas asked, "Whom shall I invite opening night who will be instrumental in attracting the greatest number of customers to Anthony's Pier 4?" Now Anthony found his answer through creative thinking. Consider the many possibilities when you ask yourself the questions. Write them down. Come to a decision as to the most desirable one. This should then be put into your permanent notebook.

4. It's imperative that you plan to inspect or check on yourself with regularity, preferably daily. Use your permanent notebook every day.

✒ Words from the Wise ✒

"Time is the most valuable thing a man can spend."
—Laertius Diogenes

"Diligence is the mother of good luck, and God gives all things to industry."—Benjamin Franklin

"You will never know what is enough unless you know what is more than enough."—William Blake

"The heights by great men reached and kept
Were not attained by sudden flight,
But they, while their companions slept,
Were toiling upward in the night."
—Henry Wadsworth Longfellow

"A sense of curiosity is nature's original school of education."—Smiley Blanton

"Nothing in life is more exciting and rewarding than the sudden flash of insight that leaves you a changed person—not only changed, but for the better."—Arthur Gordon

"For me, reading was and is a revolutionary act. It expands my mind and gives me the necessary tools for the revolution of my spirit, the revolution of my mind, and the revolution of society. . . . Choose to read, choose to learn, choose to dream."
—Bertice Berry

12

A Man Who Puts PMA to Work Every Day

The power of PMA is enormous. It can take you anywhere you want to go. It has helped countless people rise from ordinary circumstances to positions of wealth, happiness, and success.

One of the most inspiring examples of what PMA can do is W. Clement Stone, a man who has made it his business to use PMA in every possible way. His life offers a real demonstration of the impact a good, constructive attitude can have. I worked with him for nearly fifty years, and I know of no one who has put PMA to better use than Stone.

By any measure, Stone's life is a success. He has lived more than ninety- five years, seventy- five of them married to the same woman, all the while accumulating wealth, enjoying happiness, and earning the respect of his peers.

The chairman emeritus of Aon Insurance Companies, one of the largest insurance organizations in America, he is conservatively estimated to be a multi-millionaire. He has given away hundreds of millions of dollars more to charities and needy individuals.

The author of three books, Stone has also had the pleasure of sharing his ideas about PMA with thousands of people who have become rich by working for him. He is a relentless advocate of the power of positive mental action. By his words and deeds, he shows everyone how PMA can work wonders.

Let's take a look at each of the ten steps this book gives you for developing PMA, and see how W. Clement Stone has put every one of them to work. By examining his life, you can find more ways to use the power of PMA in yours.

Step One: Take Possession of Your Own Mind with Conviction

Remember the creed you were asked to adopt as part of this step? One of the most important parts of it is this:

> I believe I can direct and control my emotions, moods, feelings, intellect, tendencies, attitudes, passions, and habits with the intention of developing a Positive Mental Attitude.

Listen to what Stone has to say about the idea that you can control your mind:

I have long been an advocate of selecting thoughts and sayings that can be immediately summoned into the conscious mind to counter the negative influences we all encounter in everyday life. . . .

Since I was a teenager, I deliberately trained myself to neutralize negative suggestions from others. If someone said to me, "It can't be done," or "You can't do that," my subconscious mind would instantly flash a message to my conscious mind the positive translation: "He can't, but I can!" I practiced it so often that it became an automatic, instantaneous response.

Stone is not exaggerating. In fact, he's underplaying the real story. Born in turn-of-the-century Chicago, he lost his father when he was just three years old. His mother worked hard to support the two of them, but money was so short that when Stone was just six, he began selling newspapers on a street corner. The other newsboys were all teenagers, and their tactics were rough: they beat the young boy to drive him away.

But Stone was not stopped. He began going into restaurants and stores to find his customers: "I began to learn how to overcome fear through action." That ability to act in spite of fear is the essence of using PMA: putting the positive powers of your mind ahead of the negative forces you encounter in life.

It isn't always easy to meet a negative experience with positive thoughts and actions. That's why Stone has always made use of *self-motivators*, those catchy thoughts that you can recall instantly to add fire to your PMA.

Here are some of Stone's personal self-motivators:

- Do it NOW!
- We've got a problem—that's good!
- Aim high!
- With every adversity there is a seed of equivalent or greater benefit for those who have PMA!
- Success is achieved and maintained by those who try and keep trying with PMA!

Notice that each of these self-motivators is emphatic. They end with an exclamation point so that when Stone recalls one of them, it has a strong mental effect. This is the essence of what it means to take possession of your own mind: you choose the kind of attitude through which you evaluate everything that happens to you. As Stone says,

> If there is a single characteristic that separates successful people from those who are destined to a life of failure and defeat, it is a Positive Mental Attitude. Where a negative person sees problems, a person with PMA sees opportunities. Your future is unlimited if you choose the positive way, and when you develop a winner's attitude, you will soon discover that your income and the amount of wealth you accumulate is entirely up to you.

Step Two: Keep Your Mind on the Things You Want and off the Things You Don't Want

This step is the logical outcome of Step One, the specific application of the general idea of PMA. It requires practice and constant attention, but it offers you a twofold benefit: 1) You free yourself from worry and fear, and 2) you begin creating the situations that are necessary for obtaining those things that you want.

"Since birth, we have been conditioned to be negative," Stone admits. "We are repeatedly told what not to do or why something cannot be done. It takes a deliberate, conscious, and continuous effort to keep the negative forces under control."

As a salesman for more than ninety years (!), Stone knows what he is talking about. Every encounter he has had with a prospect has brought with it the possibility for someone to say "No!" to him. And even the best salesperson knows that this happens regularly. But the key to dealing with potential disappointment is not to dwell on the chance that you will hear "No!" Instead, you must concentrate all your thoughts on "Yes!"

"The little difference between happiness and success, and misery and failure is whether your attitude is positive or negative," Stone has often said. "Your attitude is one of the few things in life over which you have absolute and total control."

Stone offers these tips on focusing your mind on the positive whenever you enter a situation in which negative thoughts threaten to overwhelm you:

- *Be keyed up.* Concentrate on the job ahead, just as a professional athlete would concentrate on the game ahead, or an actor would concentrate on a part for the performance. You are there to win—allow yourself to experience a little of the excitement of victory in advance.
- *Be self-assured.* Know that regardless of what is said or done, a "sale" will be made. The prospect will either sell you on why he doesn't want your product or service, or you will sell him on the need for it. Enter into the "selling" situation confident in the knowledge that you will take charge of the encounter and that you will sell. If you have trouble feeling confident, begin by acting as if you were and the feeling of confidence will overtake you.
- *Relieve tension.* If you are nervous or frightened, or if you are experiencing difficulty in controlling your emotions, talk in an enthusiastic tone of voice to neutralize your emotions. Your emotions are not always subject to reason, but they are subject to *action!* One effective way to do this is to smile, and remember to smile with your eyes as well as your face. Laugh and use humor to relieve tension. This will also relieve tension on the part of other people, as they laugh or smile with you. Regardless of the feelings of others, you have the power to affect their reactions by what you say and how you say it, and by what you do and how you do it.

Stone has always been a master of this last technique. A dapper dresser who cuts a distinctive appearance, he has a trademark turned-up moustache that gives his mouth a permanent hint of a smile. He always begins a meeting, whether with a board of directors or a group of sales reps, by sharing good news, usually a list of at least five items. He takes the excitement of everything positive that has happened lately, uses it to fire up his own motivation, and then spreads that fire to everyone else in the room. He may be there to report on something that hasn't gone as planned, or to talk to a group of lackluster performers, but no matter his purpose, he starts out focusing everyone's mind on the good things that are going on; that way, he makes sure they keep on happening.

One other thing Stone does that reveals his enormous power to focus his mind: in all the years I have known him, as friend and business associate, I have never heard him greet any setback with a word stronger than "Rats." For a man with a multi-million dollar empire, who has received his share of unwelcome news that comes with having many interests, this is an amazing example of mental control.

The occasional curse word slips past almost everyone's lips at some point and is hardly a sign of mental imbalance. But they are usually uttered in a burst of anger and frustration and reveal how powerful negative attitudes can be when they surprise us. Stone's remarkable record is a testament to the degree to which his mental reactions are conditioned to stay positive in any situation.

Every time you meet a setback by staying in control of your mental attitude, it's like pushing out an extra repetition on the bench press. You are training your mind to be more fit and to do more than it has ever done before. As Stone says, PMA "is a process that must be practiced during every waking moment until it becomes a habit to greet self-doubt with self-confidence. Just as your muscles become strong and resilient through exercise and constant use, so does your mind."

Step Three: Live the Golden Rule

Do unto others as you would have them do unto you. You've probably heard this so often since childhood that your mind goes a little numb when you encounter it again. If you let this happen, you're cheating yourself of the knowledge and benefits that come from one of the most fundamental ideas behind PMA.

Throughout his long career, Stone has dealt with thousands and thousands of sales people and others who have worked for him. In his relations with all of them, he gave freely of himself, knowing that whatever it cost him in terms of time or money, he would get back in some way.

I was newly married and trying to buy my first home when I learned just how generous Stone could be. I had applied for a loan, but was turned down because I earned just thirty dollars a month too little to qualify for the mortgage. Well, I reasoned, I was close, and it wouldn't be long before I was making enough. When that happened, I figured my wife and I would find another house we liked just as much.

But word got around the company that I had met

with a setback, and I found myself summoned to Stone's office. "Mike, is it true that you were just thirty dollars a month short of getting that house?" he asked me. When I admitted it, he looked surprised, almost hurt.

"Well, why didn't you come to me? I would have been glad to help you out." And right there he gave me the raise that I needed to buy my first home.

Thirty dollars a month was hardly a fortune to Stone, but it made a huge difference to me and my wife. And though Stone had given me that money, I repaid him by working harder than ever, staying late each night, and coming to the office on weekends so that he was sure I appreciated what he had done for me.

That automatic and instant generosity has been a hallmark of Stone's life. Every once in a while an article would appear in the newspaper about a family whose house had been destroyed, or a couple from out of town whose money had been stolen. A few days later, another item would run about a mysterious benefactor who had replaced the family's clothes or paid the couple's hotel bill and bought them a ticket back home.

Those of us who had seen the look of concern when Stone had heard these stories knew that the little boy who had started working at six was usually the mysterious benefactor. It was almost like a hobby with him. "The more we earn, the more we have to share with others," he once wrote. "One thing I have learned for certain is that truly successful people make it a practice to share their wealth. They have learned from experience that when you give of yourself—when you do a good deed without any thought of reward—it gives you a wonderful feeling. And, the more you share, the more motivated you become."

Stone's application of the Golden Rule hasn't been confined to small gestures either. He has given vast amounts of money to many worthy institutions and efforts, including such diverse groups as the American Indian Center, the Boys and Girls Clubs of America, the Chicago Lyric Opera, the Massachusetts Eye and Ear Infirmary, the National Conference of Christians and Jews, and the Salvation Army.

His extraordinary success has allowed Stone to be extraordinarily generous, but behind that generosity is a way of thinking that I once heard him express very simply. Someone jokingly asked him if he wasn't afraid that some of the people he was helping were just using him to get a few fast dollars. Stone smiled and said, "I can never really know if someone who comes to me is just an opportunist or someone who has been sent by the Good Lord with a real need. But I always act as if they have come because God wants me to help them. I believe that I can never refuse to return the favors he has done me."

Perhaps you are not yet in the position to be as generous with your money as you would like. But you can give of your time, good will, and enthusiasm to those who ask—and even those who have not asked. If you deal honorably and fairly with everyone you encounter, you will confidently be able to expect that they will do the same in dealing with you.

Step Four: Eliminate All Negative Thoughts by Self-Inspection

Everyone experiences negative thoughts; it's human nature to know fear and doubt. But it is in the nature of successful people to recognize those thoughts and counteract them.

Stone's introduction to the insurance business that would bring him success was not easy. His mother had just purchased a small agency in Detroit and gave her son just one day to read over the policy they sold before pointing Stone at the huge office building across the street and telling him to start selling.

That first day, Stone sold just two policies out of countless attempts. The second day, he sold four, and the next day, six. He was improving steadily. But he still found himself hesitating each morning when it came time to enter the building. "I had not licked the fear of opening doors," he recalls:

> But, after some thinking, I reasoned 'Success is achieved by those who try. And where there is nothing to lose by trying, and a great deal to be gained if successful, by all means, try.'
>
> These self-motivators satisfied my reason. But I was still afraid. It was then necessary to get into action. Then I struck upon a great self-motivator: Do it NOW!
>
> In this manner I found I could force myself to develop the habit of getting into action. As I left one

office, I would rush quickly to the next. If I felt like hesitating, I just repeated to myself, 'Do it NOW!'

Once I was inside a place of business, I was still not at ease. But I soon learned how to neutralize my fear of talking to a stranger by using voice control. I spoke loudly, rapidly—but always kept a smile in my voice—and used modulation. Later, I learned that this technique was based on a very sound psychological principle, put forth by Professor William James of Harvard: the emotions, such as fear, are not always subject to reason, but they are always immediately subject to action. When thoughts do not neutralize an undesirable emotion, action will.

It's the same thing I was doing as a newsboy. If you get into action and keep on trying in spite of fear, this negative emotion will eventually be neutralized.

To overcome fear takes courage, endurance, and guts. Each are learned habits of thought and action. Yet even though you may not recognize it, you already potentially have courage, endurance, and guts. For when you use any of the potential powers you have, you start to develop the habit of its use. As you know, repetition develops a habit. And when you develop the habit of goal setting, endurance, firmness of mind, courage, staying power, and stamina, and persistently try for large sales, you make large sales.

Indeed, the power of repetition helps you in any worthy task that you set yourself. It programs your mind to lift you over obstacles and setbacks, and not to dwell on depressing ideas that sneak in. Still, even people who live and work in an environment with strong PMA can find themselves voicing a negative thought.

One of the easiest ways this can happen is when you allow the negative idea to take the form of a complaint about someone else. It may seem that you're staying positive—after all, you aren't saying something bad about *yourself.* But running someone else down by demeaning their work habits or anything else about them is a sign of a negative mental attitude, and you're only kidding yourself if you think it makes you look better.

Overseeing a huge sales force, Stone was often in the position of hearing employees talk about each other. Whenever he heard someone start a sentence that was designed to malign a co-worker—or even to point out a real problem—he'd say, "STOP! Find five good things to tell me about this guy, and then decide if you've got something else to say."

That technique is powerful, because it forces the person to look at the positive side of things first. Nearly every time, once five good things had been said, the bad news seemed pretty inconsequential.

The same approach will work when you find a negative thought persistently appearing in your mind. Find five good thoughts that apply to the same situation, and you'll discover that you probably can't even remember the complaint that got you started in the first place.

Step Five: Be Happy! Make Others Happy!

Happiness is tremendously infectious and attractive. If you walk into a party and see two groups of people, one laughing and smiling, the other moping and frowning, which will you want to stand near?

If you make the effort to be happy yourself, the people around you will become happy. It's a simple principle, but one that many people forget to employ. It's also easy to be happy when everything is going your way, but far more important to be happy when they aren't.

One of Stone's favorite stories is of a woman known as Grandmother Nedrow. Grandmother Nedrow lost her eyesight late in life and was initially very bitter. But she drew upon her innate PMA and made the decision to accept the physical limitation and instead change the only thing she could, her attitude.

One of Grandmother Nedrow's granddaughters told Stone, "Grandmother encouraged me to thank God each night for the good things that had happened to me that particular day, and in the morning, upon waking, to thank Him for all the good things in my life. In that way, I started each day with a feeling of well-being and contentment because rather than worrying about the things that I could not change, I actively thought about the things I didn't want to change: things that I loved, people who loved me, good fortune that had befallen me. In short, without knowing what PMA was, Gran taught me to start each day with a Positive Mental Attitude."

Stone knows how personal happiness or unhappiness

can affect every detail of a person's life. He tells the following story:

> I used the Grandmother Nedrow story to help a successful young sales manager solve his problem. He wasn't blind or in poor health, and he earned a rather large income. Most people would assume that he had everything in life that one could want. He did! But his problem was that he was unhappy without being really sure why.
>
> After a long conversation with him, it was easy to determine that his unhappiness was brought about because of the antagonism he created in others. As a sales manager he was sensitive to the possible reaction of his prospects. He attracted them. But socially and with those who worked for him, he was *insensitive*. He always seemed to be surprised at the adverse reaction that he received when he argued with people in an aggressive, thoughtless manner. They didn't like it. He repelled them.
>
> I related the Grandmother Nedrow story to him to illustrate how he could change his life if he changed his attitude. I said, 'You're great in sales! Just think how you could attract goodwill from your associates, your employees, and your social contacts if you would change your attitude toward them from negative to positive—if you were more careful about what you said and how you said it.'
>
> At first, he was defensive, a reaction that might be expected from one who is insensitive to others, but he was more interested in solving the problem than

in defending his behavior. He sincerely wanted to help himself. He asked, 'What do you recommend?'

'Use self-suggestion,' I told him. 'Repeat fifty times in the morning and fifty times at night for a week or ten days—with concentration and feeling:

- Do unto others as you would have others do unto you.
- Don't say or do unto others that which you would not want them to say or do unto you.

'You're smart enough to sell yourself by saying the right thing at the right time—by being more considerate of the feelings of others.'

Within a short time, amazing things began to happen. His associates, his employees, and his friends noticed a change. But most of all he was able to change his life from negative to positive—because he changed his attitude.

Of course, Stone's advice might not have had such a powerful effect if he wasn't such an outgoing and happy person himself. But that only illustrates one of the great benefits of being happy: you gain the power to influence others for the better.

Step Six: Form a Habit of Tolerance

A Positive Mental Attitude gives you the flexibility to get along and work with people whose views are different from your own. In our modern society, there is no short-age of issues upon which people may disagree very strongly, but that does not mean that we cannot respect each other enough to find a common cause when the stakes are high, or simply try to understand what it is that lies behind our differences.

You will frequently encounter people whose ideas differ from your own. If you cross them off your list of friends and allies, you will hurt yourself by making your world smaller. Perhaps the most common reason for friction between people is that we take their difference of opinion as a rejection of the ideas we endorse, and thus of ourselves.

Stone likes to recall the story of a young, highly motivated salesperson who called on the owner of a shoe store with the purpose of selling him insurance. She was accompanied by her sales manager, so the stakes were raised: she wanted to make a good impression on her boss.

The store owner wasn't interested in buying insurance, and said so plainly. In a burst of anger, the salesperson said, "I would never come to your store to buy a pair of shoes!"

Her reaction was understandable, but it was also undesirable and certainly not productive. Once they were out of the store, her sales manager pointed out that the store owner had given her the courtesy of his time, for which she should have been grateful. Instead, she had allowed his rejection of her product to color her attitude and thus made it impossible for her to ever call upon him again. Indeed the store owner was now likely to be very cautious about agreeing to speak to any salesperson, given his experience.

This is the broad effect that intolerant responses have: they cause both parties to put up walls. As Stone says, "If your feelings are easily hurt, then you are a person who frequently hurts the feelings of others. Your own negative thoughts cause an intensified negative force by changing the direction of the thinking of others. They align their thinking with your own negative attitude. If your feelings are seldom or never hurt, then it is a safe bet that you are a positive, optimistic person who has a depth of understanding of the feelings of others, and you will channel their reaction in the same direction."

Stone also recalls, "I learned something years ago as I sat at my desk and some salesman would be on the other side and be very angry about something, anything. I would say to myself, 'patience, patience, patience,' and not respond in a way that matched his anger. Pretty soon, he would talk himself out of it. Because the more they talked, the more they realized they were wrong. And when they quieted down, I could talk to them in a calm voice and we could solve the problem. If someone else is angry, you don't want to get angry. You want to control the situation."

Stone himself is a man of strong convictions. He has long been politically active in the Republican party. Although he works hard to support the things that he believes in, he does not let apparent differences prevent him from forming alliances with people when they can find issues of mutual interest. Does it surprise you to learn that he has supported the Reverend Jesse Jackson's Operation PUSH? It shouldn't. Stone admired Jackson for exhorting African-Americans to work hard and strive for excellence, and directed his private foundation to provide Operation PUSH with organizational management and fund-raising expertise.

That's exactly the kind of bridge that tolerance builds. Instead of thinking of himself as a conservative, white Republican, and of Jackson as a liberal, black Democrat, Stone saw that they were both men with a mission to inspire others to self-improvement. These two leaders may disagree about more things than they agree upon, but many people are better off because they ignored the differences and worked together.

Should you find yourself stumbling over your disagreements with someone, take an example from Stone's way of dealing with complaints about others, mentioned above. Ask yourself to list five good things about the person you aren't getting along with. Then ask yourself if those five things aren't enough for you to find some way of working together for your mutual benefit. That's what it takes to make tolerance a part of your PMA habits.

Step Seven: Give Yourself Positive Suggestions

If you were to find yourself introduced to W. Clement Stone and said, as you shook his hand, "How are you?" I know exactly how he would respond.

"I FEEL HEALTHY! I FEEL HAPPY! I FEEL TER-

RIFIC!" And the words would come out with all the energy and excitement those capital letters imply.

Stone is constantly giving himself positive suggestions. After a long lifetime of living with PMA, he's still reinforcing it everyday—and every night—at every opportunity. "Before I go to bed," Stone says, "I kneel down and pray that I have a deep, deep, wholesome sleep and wake up in the morning full of vim and life and vitality, and that if I dream, I have a beautiful dream and a helpful dream toward my goal."

Echoing Napoleon Hill, Stone reminds us, "What the mind can conceive and believe, the mind can achieve with PMA. We translate into physical reality the thoughts and attitude we hold in our minds. We translate thoughts of poverty and failure into reality just as quickly as we don thoughts of riches and success. When our attitude toward ourselves is big and our attitude toward others is generous and merciful, we attract big, generous portions of success to ourselves."

This is another point at which self-motivators have a powerful role to play. They can flash into your mind in a time of need—for example, when you wish to eliminate or neutralize fear, meet problems more courageously, turn disadvantages into advantages, strive for higher achievements, solve serious problems, or control your emotions.

Stone often repeats these self-motivators aloud to increase their power, and he makes sure others can hear them because he wants to spread their effects around. Og Mandino, who wrote the bestselling book *The Greatest Salesman in the World* was once the editor of *Success*

Unlimited magazine, which Stone and Napoleon Hill had founded together. He was an enthusiastic and inspiring writer, but his inexperience with production issues initially caused some problems. On one occasion, after an expensive mistake, Mandino realized that the fault was his and went to Stone to tell him what had happened.

"Og, that's terrific," Stone replied. Stone was more concerned with the fact that Mandino knew he had learned an important lesson than he was with the money the mistake had cost. He was confident that Mandino would never make the same kind of mistake again and that he would be better prepared to avoid other mistakes by realizing what he still needed to learn.

When you give yourself a positive suggestion in the face of a setback, you are taking the first step toward realizing the power of the self-motivator, *With every adversity there is a seed of equivalent or greater benefit for those who have PMA!* Stone remarks, "I'm so lucky because I have so many problems that others say can't be solved. But by PMA and keeping my mind on my goal, I am lucky because I turn that problem into an advantage."

Stone once visited a center for troubled teenagers in the Bronx where he spoke to a group of girls who had just completed a six-month job training program. The girls were excited, and nervous. None of them had ever had a job before, or even gone for an interview.

Stone told them his own story of starting out selling newspapers and how PMA had helped him become successful. He said that if the girls would learn PMA and use it, they would be able to get the jobs they wanted. "Even if you don't get the first job you go for, Positive Mental Attitude will enable you to turn that disappointment into a positive experience," he said.

"How can not getting a job be a positive experience?" one of the girls wanted to know.

"It can be a very positive experience because you will have been through a job interview," Stone replied. "The next time you will know what to expect. You will be less nervous. If you do make mistakes, you can learn from them. And the next time, or the time after that, you will do your best *and your best will be good enough*. You will know that if one employer doesn't hire you, another one will."

By the time Stone left the room, he had the girls enthusiastically shouting, "I can do it!" "Do it NOW!" and "I'm healthy! I'm happy! I'm terrific!" And soon, though not always on the first interview, every one of them had jobs.

There's nothing fake or corny about giving yourself positive suggestions. And if you don't do it, who will?

Step Eight: Use Your Power of Prayer

You've probably noticed that several of the stories above feature the use of prayer. Prayer is a highly concentrated expression of PMA, one that offers many benefits.

Stone has often praised a quotation by Sir James Mackintosh that describes an important attitude to bring to your prayers: *"It is right to be contented with what we have, never with what we are."*

Contentment with what you have does not mean that you stop striving for better things. But it does mean that you recognize and are grateful for every single good thing in your life. Consciously acknowledging these good things means you will take nothing for granted. If you offer regular thanks for your relationship with your spouse, for your good health, or for your strong friends, you will prevent yourself from overlooking and thus neglecting them.

This is why Stone never begins a business meeting, gives a speech, or makes an important decision without offering an earnest prayer. Praying connects him to the things that are most important to him. Not the making of money, but the human qualities and people that he values. Prayer has helped him operate his business and personal life by the positive principles that he holds dear, so that when a decision has to be made, it is always in accord with the things Stone knows matter most.

Many of the seemingly tough decisions we face involve a choice between two things we value, such as a business opportunity and immediate financial security. If you pray honestly, and acknowledge your principles and your situation, you will find that you will come to an understanding of whether you are ready to take a step or that you have some work to do before you take on a risk. Remember, a Positive Mental Attitude is not a blind, charge-ahead at all costs approach to living. As Stone has said, "A Positive Mental Attitude is the RIGHT honest thought, action, or reaction to a given situation or set of circumstances." Sometimes that means waiting to take a step until you are ready for it.

Prayer is a remarkably effective means of identifying and beginning to work on those areas of your life where you need to make changes. Remember Mackintosh's words: "It is right to be contented with what we have, *never with what we are.*"

Stone says, "We know that we will never reach perfection in this life, but we also know that only by striving for it do we become closer to perfection. Only those who become inspirationally dissatisfied—with PMA—can change their world and ours and make it a better place for themselves and others."

At another point, Stone once commented, "Many people pray to give thanks, and that's good, but I decided many years ago that it's not good enough. If you are really thanking the Lord, then prove it by sharing your time, your expertise, part of your wealth. Like the farmer, sow some seeds for harvest."

In other words, it is as important to act in accordance with your prayers as it is to pray. If you pray for courage, you need to behave as if it has been granted to you. If you pray for an opportunity, you need to seize it when it comes. And just as important, you should be showing your thankfulness for the blessings you have received by sharing them with others.

Stone has always done this, both by his generosity to charity and individuals, and by his determination to share PMA with as many people as possible. He was already firmly convinced of the power of a positive attitude when a friend loaned him a copy of Napoleon Hill's *Think and*

Grow Rich. Stone was so impressed with Hill's presentation of the ideas in the book that he immediately ordered a copy for each of his sales reps.

"BINGO!" Stone remembers, "I hit the jackpot. Fantastic things began to happen. . . . Many of my salesmen became supersalesmen. Sales and profits increased. Their attitudes changed from negative to positive."

But it wasn't until fifteen years later that Stone realized a way to really share the blessings of PMA. A friend invited him to a luncheon to hear Napoleon Hill speak. Though Hill was largely retired, he had agreed to come to Chicago and delivered a powerful speech. After lunch, Hill and Stone began a conversation and Stone urged Hill to come out of retirement to continue speaking and writing about PMA.

"I'll do it on one condition," Hill replied. "That you become my general manager."

And so the two men formed an alliance that would last another decade, creating films, home study courses, programs for prison inmates, and a jointly authored book. They helped thousands of people begin applying PMA.

That story is a perfect example of the readiness to show how thankful you are for the blessings you acknowledge in your daily prayers. As Stone says,

> I felt my blessings were so far beyond what any individual deserved or could have ever expected. I know I could give prayers of thanks, as I do. But I also felt I could help to do the Lord's work on earth by sharing those blessings with those less fortunate.

There are many of us who give thanks through prayers in the morning, at night, or during grace. What would happen if more of us, instead of merely praying, would act, sharing our blessings we have received, be it our experience, knowledge, ideals, or part of our wealth?

All I want to do is change the world. That's all. Can it be done? It is being done.

Step Nine: Set Goals

Throughout this book, you've repeatedly encountered the idea that PMA is not simply an attitude, but also the *actions* that apply your attitude. There is no more important step to making PMA work for you than to develop goals that you will pursue. Otherwise, it will be as if you had constructed a huge, powerful engine and forgotten to put it into a car: all the potential power at your disposal will get you nowhere.

Stone says, "A Positive Mental Attitude combined with definiteness of purpose—the selection of a specific goal—is the starting point of all success. Your world will change whether or not you choose to change it. But you do have the power to choose its direction. You can select your own targets."

Based on his long career training salespeople, Stone believes:

Ninety-eight out of every hundred people who are dissatisfied with their world do not have a clear picture in their minds of the world they would like for themselves.

Think of it! Think of the people who drift aimlessly through life, dissatisfied, struggling against a great many things, but without a clear-cut goal. Fixing a goal may not be easy. It may even involve some painful self-examination. But it is worth the effort because as soon as you can name a goal, you can expect to enjoy many advantages. These advantages come almost automatically . . .

When you know what you want, there is a tendency for you to try to get on the right track and head in the right direction. You get into action. "Action" is the key word—information and ideas without action remain dormant until applied.

You become motivated to pay the price to achieve your goal. You budget your time and money. You study, think, and plan with regularity, preferably daily, learning to recognize principles which will help you to achieve your goals and then apply them . . .

Then, the more you think about your goals, the more enthusiastic you become. And with enthusiasm, your desire turns into a *burning* desire. You will become alerted to opportunities as they present themselves in your everyday experiences. Because you know what you want, you are more likely to recognize these opportunities.

Stone has used goal-setting throughout his long record of success. But perhaps it has never been as important to him as when failure threatened not only his own business, but the entire American economy.

When the Great Depression struck, Stone's insurance company was thriving. But after a few years of steep unemployment, policy sales fell off sharply. Many of his salesmen simply gave up because they felt they couldn't make enough money.

Stone responded by setting four goals for himself:

1. Make as large an income through personal sales as possible.
2. Continue to hire new salespeople.
3. *Train* new salespeople, and those he already had, to do as well or better than Stone was himself.
4. Develop a sales-production record system that told him how much business his company was doing everywhere in the country.

These were ambitious goals, especially in a time when many businesses were failing and people wondered if America would ever know the kind of prosperity it had enjoyed just a few years before.

Stone hired Rand McNally to create the sales record system, but the other three goals were all up to him. So he set out in his car to travel the country, visiting his salespeople and going on sales calls with them, showing them his selling method. As he traveled, he would hire salespeople for new territories and spend a day with each of them, turning over that day's commissions to the new rep in order to create enthusiasm and give their PMA a boost.

Stone's business stayed solvent and began to grow again. He and his salespeople were making incomes far above what many people were scraping by on during the Depression. If he had stayed in Chicago, worried about his creditors and the loss of his sales force, that never would have happened.

You will find yourself setting short-term and long-term goals. The key to both is following through with confident actions that will translate them into reality. Don't sell yourself short.

Step Ten: Study, Think, and Plan Daily

W. Clement Stone takes baths, not showers. Showers may be faster, and wealthy people are busy people, but every morning, Stone fills his marble bathtub with steaming water and stretches out to relax. "This is a good part of my thinking time," he says.

Fired up by PMA and a burning desire to achieve your goals, you may make the mistake of thinking that you must always be doing, doing, doing. It's worthy to concentrate on action in pursuit of success, but you also need to set aside time for more contemplative efforts.

"A small drop of ink makes thousands, perhaps millions . . . think," wrote Lord Byron in his epic poem *Don Juan*. And the inspiration to new thoughts that comes with reading and studying will be important to your cultivation of PMA; you will be stimulated by new ideas and reminded of some you have forgotten.

Over the years, Stone has always been enthusiastically

recommending books he has just read to others, not only inspirational titles like *Think and Grow Rich*, but works of history, social analysis, and fiction. It's evidence of an active mind that is always trying to assimilate and relate new ideas that he can apply. It keeps his mind flexible and sharp.

Let me give you an example of how that pays off. I was a teenager working as a mail-room clerk in Stone's office, when I decided to present an idea to him. As a hobby, I had done a great deal of work with film and audio recording, and I believed that films and tapes of Stone's enthusiastic talks would be an excellent tool for our salespeople in the field.

Despite some jeers from colleagues who thought I was risking my job by writing to the president of the company, I sent Stone a memo outlining the benefits of my idea. An hour after Stone got the memo, I was called into his office. "Good to know ya, Ritt," one of the other clerks said. "Enjoy the unemployment line."

But as soon as his secretary said I was outside his office, Stone burst through the door, grabbed my hand, and said, "Great idea! Tell me more." And that afternoon we were buying equipment and setting up a new department. The techniques we used have become commonplace today, but they were revolutionary then, and Stone embraced them with enthusiasm, I believe, because he had trained his mind to be flexible and positive.

In 1979, a seventy-seven-year-old W. Clement Stone told an interviewer for *Chicago* magazine, "I'll live past eighty-seven—that's a certainty. You can extend life with

PMA." It may have seemed a boastful statement then, but now, almost twenty years later, it seems a modest assertion.

No one I have ever known or worked with better embodies the principles of a Positive Mental Attitude than W. Clement Stone. He's inspired me and thousands upon thousands of others to improve our lives. He is a great man, one who has dedicated himself to helping people and enjoyed success as a result.

I've offered you these glimpses at his life, not as a tribute, but as a practical means of showing you how PMA can truly be applied in anything you do. And how it will aid you enormously, whether you are selling newspapers, teaching moral values to your children, or running your own company.

Where you go with PMA is entirely up to you. But you can set a goal for yourself and attain it by changing only one thing about your life—*your attitude to everyone and everything that you encounter for the better.*

13

Where Do You Go from Here?

Congratulations! You've done it! As you have read this book on PMA, your mental powers have already begun to work for you. If you have been thinking in terms of your own Positive Mental Attitude and what it can and will do for you, you feel better about yourself already. And others will notice the difference—you will see new respect in people's manner as they realize that you are a person in charge of your life, in control of your feelings and attitudes.

One fact must have struck you as you read through the ten steps, and that is how integrated they are. The steps weave in and out of one another, they weave a fabric of living that is called PMA. Start to use PMA today—every day, in every way.

Where do you go from here? To a life with power and

purpose. To a life filled with the satisfaction and fun that comes from a Positive Mental Attitude. Bon Voyage!

LIVE LIFE WITH PMA: IT'S TERRIFIC!

Further Reading

The concepts, techniques, and suggestions given in this book are but the tip of the iceberg. For a complete understanding of related success principles, read, study, and apply the principles described in the following materials:

Bertice Berry. *Bertice: The World According to Me.* Scribner's. 1996.
   From life in the projects to success and fame, Berry recounts her life story with incredible inspiration and faith in God.

Dennis Conner with Edward Claflin. *The Art of Winning.* St. Martin's Press. 1988.
   Conner shows how he has used his motivational powers in all walks of life.

Stephen R. Covey. *The 7 Habits of Highly Effective People.* Fireside Books. 1990.
   Like Napoleon Hill, Covey uses examples from outstandingly successful people to show how they solve problems and exploit opportunities.

Dennis Kimbro and Napoleon Hill. *Think and Grow Rich: A Black Choice.* Ballantine Books. 1987.
Full of examples of African-Americans who have applied the principles of success in their lives.

Napoleon Hill. *Napoleon Hill's Keys to Success.* Dutton. 1994.
Step-by-step plans for developing and applying all the principles of achievement.

Napoleon Hill. *Think and Grow Rich.* Fawcett Books. 1962.
A success classic, must reading for anyone seriously intent on achieving his or her heart's desire.

Napoleon Hill. *Napoleon Hill's Positive Action Plan.* Plume. 1997.
Daily meditations for cultivating a successful, positive attitude.

Napoleon Hill and W. Clement Stone. *Success Through a Positive Mental Attitude.* Pocket Books. 1958.
This collaborative effort between Hill and Stone is *the* work for developing an in-depth understanding of the principles of successful achievement.

Susan Jeffers. *Feel the Fear and Do It Anyway.* Fawcett Books. 1987.
Dynamic techniques for overcoming self-doubts to achieve happiness.

David McCullough. *Truman*. Fireside Books. 1996.
This biography of the farmer who became President of the United States is a tribute to a man who believed in hard work and responsibility.

Bill Sands. *My Shadow Ran Fast*. The Napoleon Hill Foundation. 1995.
The inspiring story of a convicted felon who turned his life around by changing his attitude and setting worth-while goals.

W. Clement Stone. *The Success System that Never Fails*. Pocket Books. 1980.
An insight into the formula Stone developed to create PMA in his salespeople.

Terrie Williams with Joe Cooney. *The Personal Touch*. Warner Books. 1994.
Williams's philosophy for dealing with people has made her one of the most sought-after publicity professionals in the world.

Norman Vincent Peale. *My Favorite Quotations*. Harper Collins. 1990.
An uplifting collection of sayings from inspiring people.

Upon request, you may receive an autographed book-plate bearing the signature of Napoleon Hill. Address your request to: The Napoleon Hill Foundation, P. O. Box 1277, Wise, Virginia 24293. Enclose a large, self-addressed, stamped envelope. With this bookplate, you will receive a copy of Dr. Hill's famous success essays.

Index

For additional information about any of the Napoleon Hill products, please contact the following locations:

Napoleon Hill World Learning Center
Purdue University Calumet
2300 173rd Street
Hammond, Indiana 46323-2094
Judith Williamson, Director
Uriel "Chino" Martinez, Assistant
Telephone: 219-989-3173 or 219-989-3166
Email: nhf@calumet.purdue.edu

Napoleon Hill Foundation
University of Virginia-Wise
College Relations Apt. C
1 College Avenue
Wise, VA 24293
Don Green, Executive Director
Annedia Sturgill, Assistant
Telephone: 276-328-6700 or 276-328-8753
Email: napoleonhill@uvawise.edu

Website: www.naphill.org